The Epitome of "The American Dream"

Memoirs of
Werner Dreifuss

Werner Dreifuss

All profits from this book will be donated to charity.

Email address: wdreifuss@aol.com

Edited by:
 Joe Kita
 Debra Mostow Zakarin
 Dr. Jessica Cooper

A special thanks to my daughter, Marsi Dreifuss Frenkel, for doing the final editing.

All accounts, events, dates and facts described in this book are as accurate as I was able to determine.

ISBN # 13:978 1534722231
ISBN # 10:1534 722238

III

The Epitome of "The America Dream"

Memoirs of Werner Dreifuss

Dedication

This book is dedicated to my mother, Henny Dreyfuss, to the millions of Holocaust victims, and to the individuals and organizations who helped me and many others to escape from Europe.

I am eternally grateful to Sam and Leah Shapov. It was from their selfless acts of kindness that I was given the opportunity to begin a new life in America and to rebuild a family of my own ; my wife Norma, our four children, Joel, Robert, Ted and Marsi.

We have been blessed to add to our family, Joel's children, Amy, her husband Jake, and on October 29, 2016, we welcomed their new baby girl, Emerson Lee, (our first great grandchild), Joel's son Daniel, twins Jeffrey and Janine, Ted's wife, Niki and their two children Sammy and Kate, Marsi's husband Cantor Chayim Frenkel , and their two daughters, Mandi and Molli.

I also dedicate this book to all my future generations who will live because I survived.

Table of Contents

__Introduction__

For years and on many occasions, when I've shared details from the story of my life, people have said, "You should write a book." I had never given it much thought, especially because it would have taken so much time and effort.

Many years have passed and until this time I had never shared with my four children, eight grandchildren, or anyone else, my whole life story or history from my years in Europe. It was just too difficult to think about, much less talk about. Moreover, why tell such stories to your young children or grandchildren? However, as one gets older, there seems to be an urgent need to record and pass along the story of how one builds a strong character, adjust, adapt, and survive. Since coming to the United States I have persevered and accomplished more than I could ever have imagined. This too is necessary to share with others.

On a Crystal Cruise in 2013 from Los Angeles to New York, a family we knew from San Diego asked Norma and me to join them at their table for dinner. One person in particular who has known me for years while serving on a board of trustees for a charity, but knew nothing about my history, inquired about my life story. And it started to unfold. A few days later, he mentioned to me that I should write a book seeing as though I was the living example of the true "American

Dream." I had never thought about my life in such a manner. However, yes, how true it is. It has been quite a journey to achieve the American Dream.

I came to the United States in June 1941, at the age of ten, among a group of one hundred Jewish orphans fleeing from war-torn Europe. Within a week, all of us would be scattered throughout the country and most of us would never see each other again. Some of them had traveled, lived and survived with me all the way from Germany through France and finally to New York. For two years, we stayed one step ahead of the German army.

All of this was accomplished through the generosity and hard work of several organizations: Organization pour la Santé e'Education (better known as OSE), who provided homes in France, The Quakers America who paid for our passage to America, the United States Committee for the Care of European Children, and American Friends Service Committee, whom I never knew nor did they know me. I am forever grateful and indebted to the staff at the various homes where I lived.

I came without a penny to my name, not knowing a single word of English, having no family or even knowing anything about where or to whom I was going. **I was literally like a grain of sand in the wind.**

In 1961, I made a complete career change. I created from scratch a very successful business, which our oldest son, Joel, now operates. I began to diversify and expand financial endeavors without stepping on any toes. Moreover, it is the **"American dream"** that I have been fortunate enough to achieve. It's proof that anyone who has ambition, is willing to work hard and honestly, can be a great achiever.

I'm writing this book primarily for my family, but also in the hopes that it will inspire others to give back to those in need and to always strive to achieve the "American Dream"

I have been very fortunate to not be burdened by "the guilt feeling" for having survived in Europe which so many of the other orphans had for many years. Maybe it was because I was so young and found a good foster home that I was spared the feeling. Even at the young age of ten, I always lived by the creed, "never expect anything and you will never be disappointed." It has served me well.

As it is written and spoken at most Jewish High Holiday services, "to save one life is to save the world." Yes, I was saved to have my new world, my wife, four children, eight grandchildren, all their spouses and their families, my wife's family, my foster family, and many great lifelong friends, as well as my health.

It is intoxicating just to think about the new family I've created with Norma, the relationships I've kept with the children who came with me from Europe, the many friends I have made throughout my life,

I thank God for the ability to support orphaned children and aged adults who, at their stage in life, are not able to provide for themselves.

I hope you will indulge me in taking the liberty of writing about places and events from my early years and then fast-forward as many as fifty or sixty years. There have been so many occurrences that relate to one another, but happened in my life so many years apart from one another, that I felt compelled to write about them at the same time.

The more I thought about writing this book, the more integrated it became. I feel like the giant Banyan tree in Maui, Hawaii. It covers an entire block and grows sprouts from its own branches back into the earth to reconnect its roots and to support its extended branches. Or like a quilt, each patch tells its own story, but the whole story isn't complete until all of the patches are sewn together as one quilt.

As I got further into researching and writing this book, it was like plowing fallow land that had been sitting idle for so many years, only to be revived and nourished by the sun and rain.

June 21, 2016 marked the 75th anniversary of my stepping on American soil and is the ideal time to publish my life story.

When a person passes away without leaving his family and the world a recorded account of his life and his lessons learned, it is as if a library containing so much knowledge and history has burned to the ground, and this constitutes an enormous injustice to all since it is lost forever.

And the wind blew.

Cherish yesterday, dream tomorrow, and live today.

Preface

Norma, my wife of 61 years, and I are sitting outside on the 12th deck on the magnificent Crystal Serenity, enjoying a delicious lunch. We are in the middle of the Pacific Ocean on the first segment of our third Crystal World Cruise. We boarded in Miami on January 14, 2015, and for 108 days we will circle the globe.

Norma is a vision to behold against the deep blue ocean in her beautiful bright yellow, loosely knit, long-sleeve top with matching pants covering her trim body, looking much younger than her 81 years. A constant cadre of staff inquires, "Mr. Dreifuss, is there anything I might get you? Perhaps another glass of champagne? More pastries?" If ever we wanted or needed anything, their reply would be "my pleasure", and it would be taken care of immediately.

Looking out over the wide expanse of the ocean, without a ship or cloud in sight, and a gentle breeze blowing across the deck, my thoughts, as they had done on all previous cruises, drifted back to my first "cruise." It was a much different journey, at a much different time, a completely different situation, and on a very different ship, 75 long years ago.

It was June 1941, and I was crossing the Atlantic Ocean on a Portuguese tramp steamer that had been converted into a passenger ship. World War II was raging through Europe and the Germans were methodically marching across the continent. Their submarines surrounded us almost every night. Portugal, fortunately, was one of a few neutral countries at that time, so we were never attacked.

Escape was not new to me. I had been evacuated in March 1939 from an orphanage in Frankfurt, Germany called Waisenhauses, where I had lived since I was five or six years old. After "Kristallnacht" (the night of the broken glass) on November 9, 1938, I was moved to an orphanage outside of Paris. One year later in 1940, several days before the Germans invaded by going through Belgium and marching into Paris, I was evacuated to southern France to an orphanage for where I lived for approximately one year.

On my first "cruise" my mind was filled with so many questions, but no answers: Would I ever see my mother again? Would I find any relatives? What was America like? How would I and all the other orphans be accepted and treated or would we be rejected? Would we be separated from each other? Where would I live, in another orphanage or a private home? What would living in a private home be like? How would I be treated, compared to the natural born children in that family? How would I communicate, not knowing any English? What would my life be like? How would I survive? Despite all these questions, apprehension, trepidation and fears, I felt a tremendous amount of excitement and even joy. We had heard stories about America, a land of plenty, where anything was possible. Was that the truth? With so many uncertainties, I didn't dare dream of the future. I could only hope that my life would change for the better and stabilize.

Now, at the age of 85 as I am again cruising, but this time aboard the Crystal Serenity, I can't help but reflect on how I got from **there to here** and the many issues including psychological that were overcome during the intervening years. Strangely, I never recognized these issues and how they were resolved until after thinking I had finished this book. I had asked myself many questions while writing, most of which I was able to answer except one. What was my motivation and drive? The answers came to me in the middle of the night on the 2016 World Cruise.

You will meet many of the people who have been an intricate part of my life, many of whom, sadly, have passed away. This is the story of how that shy, scared little 10 year-old boy got from **there to here** and the many memorable events, both joyful and sad, that occurred along the way.

Come to think about it, I didn't even have to pay for that first "cruise" and yet it was the ticket to a new life.

"Yes, please, maybe I will have another glass of champagne."

Chapter 1-Waisenhauses

It was a large, gray, old, four-story, L-shaped building with a dirt playground that had a sand box in the middle. There was a tall, wood plank fence on one side with a vegetable farm on the opposite side. The top floor of the building had a retractable roof, so it would open to make a Sukkah for Sukkoth, the Jewish festival of harvest. When closed, the room was used for other Jewish holidays and events.

My earliest recollection as a child was living there, a Kosher Jewish orphanage in Frankfurt, Germany with about 70 other children. I have no recollection of the exact age I was when I arrived there. I must have been between 5 and 7 years old. I was born March 12, 1931.

Waisenhauses 1938

Werner Dreifuss (left) and a boy named
Norbert, 1938

Tante Rena, a caretaker, and eight-year-old Werner
Waisenhauses 1939

Photo album given to me by Tante Rena before
evacuating to France, 1939

Page one of the photo album, Tante Rena
wishing me well and my signature*
*Note: I signed my last name with an "i" instead of
"y" and continued signing that way.

Werner Dreifuss front row 4th from right

Lighting Hanukah candles. Werner (4th from right front row) and Fred Strauss* (2nd from left front row)

*Name on the walls chapter 2.

Summer camp while at Waisenhauses

Werner Dreifuss (in white shirt front row on the left), Hermann Bacharach, known as DUDU (third row over my left shoulder with no shirt, the big boy), Cilly Levitus (over his right shoulder, the girl with long pig tails) and Elfriede Meyer (second girl to DUDU's left).

Cilly, DUDU, Elfriede and Henry Schuster, who came to the orphanage after the above picture was taken, were all friends at Waisenhauses and about 14 to 15 years old and stayed in touch with each other all their lives. You will read more about them throughout this book.

I was told that my mother, Henny Dreyfuss, lived in Darmstadt, Germany, and worked in a bakery. I assume that is where I was born, as it is noted in all the travel

5

documents. Because of her work and bad financial conditions, she was unable to care for me.
I have a very faint recollection of her visiting me on several occasions. I was content at Waisenhauses since I never remembered living anywhere else.

Being one of the smallest children, I always looked up to the older, larger kids and that must have given me an inferiority complex.

Henny Dreyfuss
My mother left me with her picture and several of me, one as an infant and one at the age of five or six years old.

Werner Dreifuss in Germany

Life as I remember was good at the home where Tanta Rena was one of our caretakers. We were well cared for, went to summer camp and celebrated all the Jewish holidays.

All was well at the home until Kristallnacht on November 9, 1938, when mob violence broke out throughout Germany all while the regular police stood by and crowds of spectators watched. German storm troopers and Nazi youths attacked and beat Jewish people, burned synagogues (including desecrations of sacred Torah scroll), broke windows, looted and destroyed their stores and buildings.

7

It was a terrible time for all, especially for an eight year old. I remember being very scared. Fortunately, nobody got hurt nor was fire set to the orphanage. We could see smoke rising from the burning synagogues in the distance.

In March of 1939, we were asked to pack in a hurry. This didn't take long since I had very little to pack, a few pieces of clothing, and the small photo album that Tanta Rena had given me, the three pictures from my mother, and pictures taken while at Waisenhauses. I was on my way to France with a group of 11 children, including Elfriede, Henry, and DUDU, and with one adult escort, Frau Marks. I was separated from many of my friends at the orphanage.

I will never know how or why I was selected to go to France instead of Israel, Holland (where Cilly and one of her sisters was sent in a group of 24 girls in November 1938), Switzerland, Belgium, or England, where the other children were sent. The photo album, the few pictures and the memories of a little boy living in an orphanage is all that remains of my life in Germany.

The world would never be the same. Everything was happening so fast with all the Jews trying to escape Germany and other countries the Germans had occupied. Our whole world was in turmoil. The life of the Jewish people in Germany, as well as the rest of Europe, was going downhill. Six million Jewish people, including my mother, were exterminated because of one person whose name I will not even mention.

I was very fortunate to have been evacuated and to have escaped the Holocaust.

I never again heard from my mother after leaving Frankfurt.

Chapter 2-The French Connection

In early 1934, thanks to the generosity of Baroness Pierre de Gunzburg, a day home for about 30 Jewish children was established. It became part of Organization pour la Santé et I 'Education, better known as OSE, originally founded in Russia in 1912. That was the first of many French homes to care, house and save Jewish children from all over Europe. In 1935 a branch was formed in Berlin, Germany as well as in Paris, France, where OSE made their world headquarters. The biggest expansion and establishment of homes happened from the end of 1938 through 1939. Many large properties were acquired by OSE all over France to house all the children fleeing Germany and other occupied countries.

How can I ever forget what they did for all the others and me?

I owe them a great debt of gratitude for providing everything to sustain my life as well as many others in France for two years including shelter, food, (which many times was very scarce) clothing and the transportation from Paris to Limoges and then through Spain and finally to Lisbon in 1941. Until this day, OSE remains very active in helping Jewish people in need and is supported by people all over the world, including myself.

The first place we stayed in France was an old monastery. It was out in the country, which was a refreshing change from the city of Frankfurt. It was just a temporary place to stay for several weeks until accommodations became available at Villa Helvetia, at Montmorency, one of OSE's homes about 10 miles east of Paris near Eaubonne. It was here that Oswald Kernberg (now Art Kerns), who had come from Austria, and I first met. He was four years older than I.

He and I were transferred to Eaubonne with the other Orthodox children, including those who came with me from Waisenhauses to Villa de la Chesnais at 1 Avenue Voltaire. It became the orphanage for the Orthodox children.

The Chateau had been the family home of one of the wealthy DuPont's from the DuPont Company that was either rented or loaned to the OSE.

Everything was happening so fast with all the Jews trying to escape Germany and other countries the German's had captured.

We were in a new country and didn't know any French or if Germany and France were going to war against each other.

Villa Helvetia at Montmorency

As you can see from the picture above, OSE was very desperate to find facilities large enough to house the onslaught of refugees coming into France.

Germany and France had signed a treaty not to go to war against each other so it seemed France was a safe refuge for us. The French had built The Maginot Line, a major fortification between the two countries that seemed impregnable and would keep the Germans out.

However, in June of 1940, Germany invaded Poland. France and England declared war against Germany and our whole world again went into chaos.

Front steps Chateau de la Chesnais 1939

Werner on the same steps 2001

Soon after war was declared, Germany started bombing Paris, mostly at night. There were very few nights that we didn't spend in the air raid shelter.

Before our gas masks arrived, we were told to take our handkerchiefs and, if gas bombs were dropped, to soak them in vinegar and put them over our mouths. We were lucky and never had to use them nor were we hit by the bombs that we heard almost every night.

Charlotte*, Werner, and? France 1939-40

Back L-R) DUDU, Henry,"Fritz" Strauss (names on the wall)*

Front –Elfriede and Werner France 1939-40

* Charlotte and I met again at the OSE reunion in1989

When the gas masks arrived, they were placed on a shelf leading down from the dining room into the basement and we picked up ours on the way to the shelter.

When the air raid sirens sounded at night, we had to put on our coats and shoes, both of which we always placed at the end of our beds, and go to the shelter. The older children were responsible for seeing that we younger children put on our things and got there. Once down in the shelter I, along with the other younger children, sat on old mattresses on the floor. Sometimes we were given candy bars and taught to sing the French national anthem, which I still remember.

There was a single light bulb hanging from the cciling. The room was cold and musty. I was always scared and feared that if the building was bombed, there would be no escape. We were not allowed to go to sleep in case we had to evacuate. We were told never to eat or touch any items found in the surrounding lawns and trees, as they might have been dropped by the Germans and be poisoned or explosives.

That never happened, but sometimes we found old military shells that turned out to be from World War I. Even after spending part of almost every night in the air raid shelter, we were required to attend school the following day. The school was a large, modern, two-story building. It was difficult trying to learn French because we were always tired and only spoke German at the orphanage. I remember being in a class where they were using matches to teach math. I thought that was for little kids and ran back to the orphanage. I also recall being in some kind of play in which I wore a bunny suit and hopped around the stage wearing some kind of sign. I did learn a little French.

One weekend the air raid sirens sounded in the early afternoon and we were in the shelter until evening. It was the first daytime air raid. Within a few days, the German army marched through Belgium, which surrendered almost immediately, not wanting their country to be destroyed, and right into France. There was very little defense between the Belgium and French border.

The OSE had hired an Austrian Jewish educator, Ernest Papanek, who had fled to France in 1937 with his wife, and became the director of the orphanages. His wife was a doctor and was in charge of our health. They, and the OSE, did a fantastic job despite all adversities. The OSE made miracles happen literally one after the other.

Mr. Papanek and his wife, who were on the German's most-wanted list, were able to flee to the US about the same time that I did. They continued to work with orphanages in New York and wrote many articles and books, including *Out of the Fire,* which has this picture of him getting a surprise birthday cake as a group of children watched, one of who was I.

Werner (with black cap) is to the left of a girl
in a black dress on right side of picture.

Close up of Werner Dreifuss (black cap) in middle.

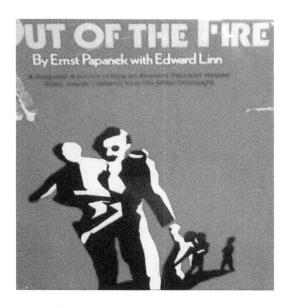

OUT OF THE FIRE

By Ernst Papanek with Edward Linn

As I mentioned before, the OSE committee, which was sponsored by Baroness Pierre de Gunzburg and by the American OSE in New York, financed the OSE. But that was not enough. The major part came from the Joint American Jewish Distribution Committee, which involved complicated manipulations, since American money couldn't be sent directly to France. The Quakers of America were instrumental transferring funds.

Marshall Fields, a storeowner in Chicago, was very active in financing and directing our survival. The money must have come via Switzerland or Lisbon. People would transport gold in cars with false bottoms

18

while others would carry wads of banknotes under their saddlebags on their bicycles to pay the bills of the orphanages.

On May 10, 1940, the French government surrendered to Germany and an armistice was signed on May 19, 1940, whereby the southern part of France was to remain under control of the French Vichy government.

On June 7, 1940, the German troops were ready to enter Paris. A few days before, approximately 100 of the younger children from the homes were taken to one location. We were all afraid that German troops would capture us. The entire city seemed to be fleeing to southern France by any available mode of transportation. It was sheer panic.

By some miracle, the OSE was able to obtain enough space on a train for all the children under the age of 16 to go to Limoges. We were evacuated in private cars to the train station in groups of four to six, which in itself was also a miracle since the streets were so crowded with people walking, driving, on bicycles, pushing wheel barrels or horse drawn wagons filled with life-long possessions and treasures. The train itself was covered with people on top and outside. It had to travel at a very slow speed since the tracks and the crossings were a solid wave of fleeing humans. French and English soldiers were fleeing the city to the English Channel at Dunkirk where British ships rescued them.

The roads along the train tracks were a solid wave of people with abandoned vehicles pushed to the sides that had run out of gas, and lying everywhere from the strafing of German planes were many dead bloody bodies and crying children next to them.

I was only nine years old. However, I will never forget that scene.

The children, 16 and older, including Art Kerns, had to obtain special papers and OSE acquired a truck with a full gas tank (another miracle), and they were able to join us a few days later at Montintin.

Again, the photo album, the few pictures and of course the memories of a little boy living in two orphanages is all that remains of my life in Germany and now in Eaubonne.

Fast forward:

In 2001, our youngest son, Ted, was working in Amsterdam and living in Laren, where he met Niki. She was working for Nike as an event planner. They planned to marry on July 14, 2001, Bastille Day, in Tours, Southern France.

Norma and I flew to Paris a few days prior to the wedding with hopes of visiting the DuPont Château in Eaubonne and doing some sightseeing. We had the address, thanks to Art Kerns, but had no idea as to who owned it or if it was even still there. We arrived in Paris late in the afternoon on a Sunday, checked into

our hotel and had dinner. We planned on going to
Eaubonne first thing the next morning.

With the time change and long flight, we didn't
wake up until 1 o'clock on Monday afternoon. We
decided to go to Eaubonne anyway. After eating, we
acquired written directions at the front desk of our
hotel as to how to get there on underground trains. We
got to the underground and it was like an anthill with
all the different levels, trains coming and going in all
directions, and signs only in French. We showed the
directions to a nice African French man, who actually
took us to our platform, which was several levels below.
A woman standing there told us not to take the train
coming but the one after. We found them all to be
extremely helpful.

When we got to Eaubonne we found a cab (I think it
was the only one in town), and showed the driver the
address. He left us off at a large eight-foot locked iron
gate with a long gravel driveway. I could see the
Chateau in the middle just as I remembered it. There
were several cars parked by the side, so we assumed
someone was there. I asked the driver if he could wait
in case there was no one home, but he said he had to
go. There was no bell so we walked around the block to
see if there was another entrance, which we found on
the side. I rang the bell for a few minutes. There was a
dog barking, but no response. Then, all of a sudden, a
young man carrying a backpack over his shoulder came

21

out of a side door, which was about 50 feet from the gate.

I was standing on the stone fence, which was about two feet high with a wire fence on top and started to call to him in French, waving my arms and he came toward the gate. I asked, "Do you speak English?" He replied, "Yes." Thank G-d, I thought.

He let us in and I informed him that I had lived there in 1939 and asked what his position was. He said he owned the Chateau. We asked if it was possible for us to go through and see it. He happily replied yes. He seemed very interested in learning about the history of the Chateau.

I asked why he was home on a Monday afternoon. He told us his wife just had a baby a few days earlier and he decided to stay home that day. Now, was that meant to be?
Again, timing in life is everything.

He was so pleased to hear my story and wanted to know all about how it was when I lived there. He said he did not even hear the bell or the dog barking but was on his way to town to get something for his wife.

His name was Liv Soavina and he worked for a telecommunications company in Paris. Mr. DuPont had died and his wife moved away and the building was going to ruins. It went up for sale and Liv bought it. Because it is a historical monument, he had to restore it to the original look, which he had been doing as he could afford it. They rent it out for parties and all kinds of occasions, and it was going to be a hotel when all the rooms were refurbished.

He showed us the grounds, which he already had redone, and they were as beautiful as I remembered them. Then he took us through the Chateau. Some rooms were still in the process of restoration. To tell the truth, I did not remember too much of the interior.

The last thing he showed us was the cellar. This was the part of the Chateau I remembered as if it was yesterday. It was still cold, damp, and had a musty smell. There was a shelf by the stairs where our gas masks use to be. There had not been any restoration done. The first room he showed us was where the younger kids, including myself, would sit on mattresses and learn the French national anthem. Liv was using it as a tool room.

I also remembered a room filled with empty wine racks and bottles and one with a large heating oil tank. These two rooms were the same as they were the day we evacuated in 1940.

Then Liv took us to another room that I did not even know existed. It was in the middle of the cellar and had no windows. He moved stacks of empty boxes away from the walls, and there on the walls were the names of many of the older children, many of whom I knew and some of whom I have pictures of. Most of the names appeared as if they had been written that day. Here it was, over 60 years since the older children had occupied this room during the air raids. The names had never faded, peeled or been painted over. I went goosy all over when I saw them. It was unbelievable.

Before we left home, I had changed backpacks and my camera was left at home in the pack. All I had with me was a throwaway Kodak camera, which I knew would not do justice to the names. Liv promised he would take pictures and e-mail them, which he did. I am ever so grateful to him. I told Liv that I knew of a picture taken of the front of the Château that Elfriede had, and I would e-mail him a copy, which I did. Afterwards, he invited us to have tea and cake with him and drove us back to the station. We still keep in touch.

Liv Soavina and Werner by the stairs to the cellar 2001

Norma and I at a statue that was there in 1939, me at the gate, Liv, the current owner and me, front and rear of the Chateau, July 12, 2001.

His nickname DUDU on the wall   Hermann Bacharach bar Mitzvah. Born January 26, 1926.

Fred (Fritz) Strauss, second from left page 7, came over with me on the first transport.
He was born September 14, 1926, lived in New Jersey and passed away in 2013.

I sent them to all the people that I was in contact with and they forwarded them to all their contacts. Just think of the fact that if I had not seen these walls, which had no meaning whatsoever to Liv at that time, and gotten the pictures, they would have been lost forever.

Again, timing in life is everything.

http://ChateaudeLaChesnaie.free.fr

Chapter 3 Montintin

It was midnight when we arrived at Limoges and boarded buses to Montintin, our new home in a remote area about 13 miles away. We were all tired and hungry. There were no beds or furniture so we slept on the floor for a few nights. A few days later, the beds from the homes near Paris arrived. OSE again had performed a miracle.

There were two buildings. The main Chateau Montintin originally was a castle and had been remodeled over the years, and the Chevrette had been the servants' quarters. It was to the right and up a slight hill from the main house and housed most of the Orthodox children. There were no toilets in the Chevrette, only an outhouse, so we younger ones slept in Chateau Montintin. Some of the older children, including Henry Schuster, who had learned woodworking in Eaubonne, started building tables, benches, shelves, etc. The home was in a wooded area so there was plenty of lumber and it was a great place to play. There were three very tall pine trees near the front of Montintin that the athletic director, Ludi, climbed and tied a bandana on top and then challenged the older kids to climb up and retrieve it.

Food was very scarce and we would hunt for berries in the woods. Rabbit was the only meat available so there was no choice, other than to go hungry. Fresh French bread was delivered by a horse-drawn wagon. Henry Schuster would ride his bicycle to a local farm and bring back milk. There were apples from the orchards around the home, which we baked on the hot stovepipe in our large bedroom on the third floor. There was a large passageway surrounding the outside of the bedroom. We never figured out what it was made for, but it was fun for hiding.

Except for the food shortage, there were no signs of the war. There was no air raid shelter, which was very unusual. Finally, we felt safe and at ease.

Thanks to pressure from the Jewish and Quaker organizations, as well as Mrs. Eleanor Roosevelt and Marshall Fields, in May 1940, the United States issued 300 visas for orphaned children, These visas were originally issued for Jewish children in internment camps, but it turned out to be too difficult to get them out of there, so they were transferred to OSE children.

100 children chosen (of which I was one) to go to America on the first transport in June of 1941 were either orphans or children whose parents' whereabouts were unknown. There were two additional transports of 100 children before America entered the war.

Fast Forward:

In 2001, after Ted and Niki's wedding in southern France we tried to visit Montintin, now a gated area and known as "the castle, but we were refused by the owner. We stayed in town for an extra night and went to the tourism office the next day in hopes they would have luck arranging for us to visit the Castle. But to no avail. You win some and you lose some.

Chateau Montintin originally was a castle 1940

The Chevrette, which had been the servants' quarters, 1940

Before leaving Montintin in 1941 to go to America, my friend Art Kerns gave me a small composition book. It was filled caricatures he had drawn, and short funny stories he had written to keep me entertained on the ship. We lost contact from that time on. He came to the US on the second transport. I kept the book, but over the years had forgotten who gave it to me.

Fast Forward:

On a Saturday afternoon in 1963, we were living on College Gardens Court in San Diego, when a man came to the door, speaking with a thick German accent. He asked Norma if Werner Dreifuss lived here. It was Art Kerns with his wife Trudie and their three children from Los Angeles. They were in San Diego for the weekend and found my name in the phone book. They stayed for dinner. Afterwards, I showed him the composition book and asked him if he knew who gave it to me. As you might guess, he was the one. I gave it back to him and asked him to make me a copy, which he did.

Fast Forward:

A few years ago, we were visiting our daughter, Marsi, and son-in-law, Cantor Chayim Frenkel, who had some doings at the Jewish Museum of Tolerance in Los Angeles. Chayim asked if I wanted to accompany him, which I did. Lo and behold, there was the book along with other collectibles that Art Kerns had donated to the museum.

31

Since that time in 1963, thanks to Art, I have reconnected with many old contacts. Art and Trudie have had many get-togethers at their home in Los Angeles. They both were instrumental in organizing a two-day reunion of the OSE children, held on March 25 and 26, 1989. Many years ago Art was very active in obtaining copies of the children manifest passenger list of the Mouzinho, as well as copies of the official correspondence that arranged for us to be onboard.

On June 27th, 2004, Norma and I had our 50th wedding anniversary celebration at the Westgate Hotel. Art and Trudy were there with us, as well as, Rosalie (Blau) Johnson, her husband Hal from Los Angeles, and Elfriede and Ed Schloss from San Diego,

Pages from Art's book

Top - Ludi and other staff at the OSE homes

Chapter 4
A Scene Never Forgotten

On June 1, 1941, we traveled from Montintin by buses to the train station in Limoges. It was a trip with mixed emotions; joy for going to America and sadness for leaving many friends with no assurance they would follow us or if I would ever see them again.

The train was typical European with individual compartments but no luxury section. The benches were a light wood and looked like new. However, they were very uncomfortable. The luggage racks above were the same type wood as the benches. Since we didn't have much luggage, the racks were filled with three foot-long loaves of French bread for us to eat on the way through Spain and then to Lisbon.

A few of the children living at Montintin had parents at an internment camp (later it turned into a concentration camp with few survivors) in Grus, France. Special arrangements were made to bring the parents to the train station at Oloron, under police, escort, to see their children. It is extremely difficult to describe the scene at the station platform. The children were permitted off the train for a few minutes. Picture, if possible, children who could hardly recognize their parents or speak to them since some had forgotten their native German. The children had refused to eat breakfast on the train that morning but wrapped up the bread, rolls and bits of sugar to give to their parents. It was very emotional since the parents knew this would probably be the last time they would ever again see their children.

I remember it was one boy's birthday and his mother gave him a tin can containing a coin as a gift. I could literally feel the restraint of the parents not to cry, but to no avail. Many, many tears were shed during this final encounter.

We handed the hungry parents, through the windows, all the bread and jams they could carry from the supply we had stacked in the luggage racks. I will never forget that scene and still get tears just thinking or writing about it. The train ride was very quiet for some time after that. One learns compassion even at such a young age.

We made use of the empty racks for the smaller children including me, to sleep on. They were just as uncomfortable as the benches.

At the Spanish border, we transferred to a Spanish train that seemed ancient, but had upholstered benches that were much more comfortable. We stopped overnight in Madrid and were taken to a Catholic convent where we had our first hot meal in days. The next day we continued on buses to Lisbon. Except for the beautiful snow-covered Pyrenees Mountains and many tunnels, Spain looked like a wrecking yard with abandoned military items and damage from the Spanish Revolution and Civil War from 1936 to 1939.

After four nights and five days of travel, we arrived in Lisbon. A group of women greeted us with candy and fruit. Some of the children ate so much they got sick. Others stashed away all they could because they were afraid they would never see so much food again.

They housed us at a school, which was vacant for summer vacation. It was across the highway from the beach, had a big play area, a kitchen and dining area, and they brought in beds for us.

We were all taken to see a movie and then to lunch at a hotel that had an indoor swimming pool. I had never seen a swimming pool before, let alone one inside a hotel. The weather was fantastic.

It took two weeks for all the paperwork, much of which I have copies of, to be completed and for money to be sent by Quakers America for our passage fare.

Werner Dreifuss left front, Portugal June 1941

Chapter 5
My First "Cruise" The S.S. Mouzinho

Corcovado, as it was known from 1908, was purchased in 1929 by CCN (Companhia Colonial de Navegacao) and baptized with the name of S.S. MOUZINHO.

We were 100 orphaned children onboard, some caretakers and, of course, the regular passengers who had the first and second-class accommodations. We ate in second class and slept in no class, in the hull.

We left Lisbon on June 10, 1941 and arrived in New York on June 21, 1941.

The Mouzinho was nothing like the many luxury ships Norma and I have cruised on in the last forty-some years including the Crystal, Oceania, Silver Seas and others, especially in size, sleeping accommodations, service (no private stateroom verandas with room service, for sure), food, entertainment (there was none for us), and most of all, peace of mind.

Fast Forward:

We were all given a picture postcard of the Mouzinho but somehow I thought it had gotten lost at the "ranch" some 65 years ago. In 2010, I was online checking some information about the ship and a link came up with the postcard of the MOUZINHO for $12.50 at a resale shop in Lisbon. It was sent in 1936 to someone in Lisbon. I was happy to buy it.

This is hard to believe. As I have been plowing through our whole house for material for this book and finding pictures and other items I had not seen in years, I found the original post card.

The food was good and plentiful, especially compared to Montintin. The third- class (?) sleeping quarters were in the hull of the ship. It had been converted from cargo space into one large room (steerage) with bunk beds for the children and the few chaperones.

It was dark and cold. I was in a top bunk and afraid to get out of bed all night, even to go to the bathroom. We slept there and spent the days on the deck. I never got seasick. We had a lot of fun playing hide-and-seek, however, we and the other passengers were in constant fear that Germany would declare war on Portugal. We would be sitting ducks for the German submarines circling the ship at night.

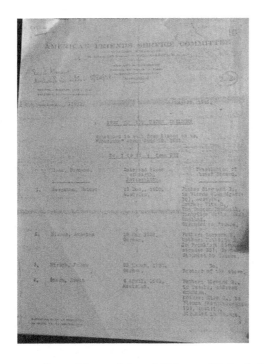

Page one of manifest of the children. #3 Jack Hirsch

List of 100 German Children, Part 2.

Name, Surname.	Date and Place of Birth. (Nationality.)	Translation of Brief Record.
5. Mr, Albert	26 Feb., 1927, German.	Father: Robert W., Mother: Hilde A., in Schweinfurt, Germany. Stranded in France.
6. Mr, Martin	30 Jan., 1931, German.	Do. Brother of the above.
7. Miller, Joseph	22 Dec., 1927, Austrian.	Father: Emile A., Friedrichstr. Miller & Co., Dept. North Ireland. Mother: Chaja B., in Vienna. Stranded in France.
8. Onem, Berthold	3 May, 1933, German.	Father: Fritz d., Mother: Else D. In Germany. Aunt: Mme Margot John, Maison d'enfants, Marsel. Stranded in France.
9. Cold, Hans	7 May, 1922, German.	Do. Brother of the above.
10. Dreyfuss, Werner	12 March, 1931, Belgian.	Father: deceased. Mother: Henny D., address unknown. Guardian: Mr. Mayer, former Director of the Transport Orphanage. Stranded in France.
11. Grunebaum, Erich	7 Feb., 1928, German.	Father: Louis A., and Mother in Fürth ..., Germany. Aunt: Mrs. Marx, c/o Rabbin Deutsch, Avenue Georgette, Limoges D./., France. Stranded in France.
12. Herschel, Walter	28 Dec., 1928, German.	Father: deceased. Mother: Ma. B., in Bad Kreuznach (Rhineland) .... Stranded in France.

Page two*, #10 Werner, # 11 Eric Grunebaum now Eric Greene, and #12 Walter Herschel, (more about them later)

   *Copies of these documents, as well as many others were obtained years ago, through the efforts of Art and Trudie Kerns of Los Angeles.

L-F Henry Schuster, L-T Werner and others on the
ship June 1941

Again, I came with all my few prior possessions and
past memories.

Chapter 6
♫ We're Coming to America ♫

The numbers on the manifest were the same as the one each of us had to wear on a tag when arriving in New York in case we got lost.

*"Coming to America" was composed and sung by Neil Diamond in the 1980 movie "The Jazz Singer." We will reconnect in Chapter 44.

It was a very hot day when we arrived and I had taken off my green tweed jacket and left it on the ship. I was very upset at not being able to retrieve it.

I had mixed emotions. I was very happy to be in America, but also sad, knowing I would soon be separated from my friends, most of whom I would never see again. Also having to learn a new language, not knowing how, where or to whom I was going was exciting as well as scary.

Of the 11 children evacuated from Waisenhauses in Frankfurt to France in March 1939, four of us, Henry, Elfriede, Hermann, and I, stayed together all through France for two years and came to the USA on the first transport, only to be separated and sent to all parts of America.

On arrival at New York, a few relatives and many more reporters greeted us, since this was the first such occasion of Jewish orphans coming to America. We were taken to a Jewish orphanage at 37th and Amsterdam Street and, from there, sent to various parts of the United States. Henry (Heinz) Schuster was sent to Shreveport, LA, Elfriede (Meyer) Schloss to Chicago and Hermann (DUDU) Bacharach, to Maryland, NY and me to California. I never saw DUDU again. I Googled DUDU and found that he died November 1, 1968 at the age of 43 and was buried at Fort Benning Cemetery, GA. He was a Sergeant First Class E7 in the US Army.

Chapter 7
♫ California Here I Come ♫*

I was among 15 children, including #12 Walter Herschel and #81 Rosalie Blau, on the ship passenger list chosen to go to an orphanage in Los Angeles by way of a Pullman train. It took about one week. Why Los Angeles, I don't know. Maybe that was the only place that had room for us.

The train ride, which included many stops, was great, especially the Pullman beds, which were heaven compared to the bunk bed in steerage in the bottom of the Mouzinho and the trains in France and Spain. The food was great. We also enjoyed the scenery along the way.

*"California Here I Come" was written by Buddy De Sylvia and Joseph Meyer and made famous by Al Jolson in 1924.

Chapter 8
Vista Del Mar Orphanage #4

From the train station in downtown Los Angeles, we were bussed to Vista Del Mar. I remember going by a drugstore that had a large round red Coca Cola sign. I didn't know what Coca Cola was, but the sign seemed so impressive.

Vista Del Mar, an orphanage, opened in 1910 to care for Jewish orphans and children in need. It has grown and moved several times over the years and now is located at 3200 Motor Avenue in the Palms area of Los Angeles. The facility provides services for children with special needs and learning disabilities.

At the time the facility consisted of five, large two-story houses with room for 18 children in each and a housemother. There were three houses on one side of the street, two across with an administration building on the right, a synagogue on the left, as well as Mr. Bonaparte's (the director's home), the laundry, and a chicken coup. Past the houses at the end of the street were a gymnasium and a picnic area.

I was the only one of our group placed in house #32. It was across from the administration building. Everybody had chores to do. One of the kids gave me a note to get some "elbow grease" and motioned me to go to the administration building. They all had a good laugh when I came back. This didn't help my self-esteem.

The administration building   Werner at Vista Del Mar
1942

I remember one of the older children coming from the administration building in the late afternoons selling candy bars out of a glass-topped box with a carrying strap around his neck. Some of the older American children did extra work at the home, for which they were paid. Many received money from their relatives who visited and were able to buy candy. I never had any money, so I couldn't buy candy.

We all were available for adoption or to go live in a foster home.

The Cohens from Beverly Hills, who were childless, adopted Rosalie Blau, and brought Rosalie's sister from Europe after the war.

One weekend Sampson and Bernice Weinschenk, a very nice Jewish couple, took me out. They lived upstairs in a deluxe four-plex in Los Angeles, where I had my own bedroom for the first time in my life that weekend. They had a daughter, Beverly, about 18 years old, and owned an electric appliance and service business. We went out to dinner and then Sampson took me to a wrestling match, the kind they have on TV. I thought that one of the wrestlers was dead at the end of one match.

The Weinschenks wanted to adopt me and although I really wanted to get out of the orphanage, I declined because they were not Jewish enough. There was no Mezuzah on their front door and no Sabbath candlesticks and I didn't want to live in the city. I recommended they adopt Walter Herschel, which they did. I never heard from him again and he never attended any of the reunions.

I wasn't aware of any difficulty in the process of adoption by couples that were childless or wanted children in their homes.

I started grammar school in Palms without any problems. I had no choice but to learn English quickly, since there was no one in my house who spoke German.

On December 7, 1941, Japan attacked Pearl Harbor and America declared war on Japan and Germany. I remembered when France and England declared war on Germany and thought here we go again, being bombed by Germans. However, I was assured there was a big ocean separating us, and it would never happen here.

Items such as gasoline, tires, butter, meat and shoes were all rationed. Any item that was needed for the war effort to help build aircraft, trucks, tanks, ammunition, etc. was bought at collection centers.

There was a city dump several blocks from the picnic area of the home and several friends and I went there to search for old rubber balls and other items to sell at the collection center. With that money, I was finally able to buy candy and even War Saving Stamps. When you had $18.50 worth of stamps, they could be redeemed for a War Bond that would be worth

$25.00 in ten years. I never even came close to having enough stamps for a bond.

One afternoon I saw a big cloud of smoke coming from the direction of our grammar school and where we bought our War Saving Stamps. I had purchased some several days before and left them in my school desk. There goes my big (maybe $1.50 worth) life's savings, I thought. Much to my relief, the smoke was not from the school.

Fast Forward:

Across from house #32 lived a kid named Marvin Zigman, as well as his older brother and sister. My wife, Norma, and her girlfriend, Irene, lived in Los Angeles as teenagers and did volunteer office work at Vista Del Mar. The children from the orphanage attended Hamilton High School. Norma also happened to go there and had classes with Marvin as well as later at UCLA. A few years after Norma and I got married, we learned that Marvin and his wife, Bebe, who Norma also knew from UCLA, had moved to San Diego and we renewed our friendship.

Sometime near the end of 1942, the head of the orphanage, Joseph Bonaparte, called me to his office to meet a couple, Sam and Leah Shapov, who had come to foster or adopt a boy of about my age. No reason was given to me as to why they were specifically interested in fostering a child my age.

They were the complete opposite of the Weinschenks. They seemed much older, drove an older car (not a fancy one like the Weinschenks), and didn't appear well to do.

They took me out for several days visiting Leah's family in Los Angeles, including her brother, Rabbi Nathan Addleson, and his wife Anna. They told me that they lived on a ranch in Chula Vista, south of San Diego, and all about the many animals there. It sounded a lot better than staying in the orphanage and I was eager to join their family.

However, things were very quiet driving back to Vista Del Mar and when we arrived Sam said they wouldn't be taking me, dropped me off, and started to drive away. Leah never said a word.

Chapter 9
Sam and Leah (Addleson) Shapov

Sam Shapov was born in Lithuania on April 23, 1897 and came to America as a young man. He enlisted in the Army at age 22 during the First World War and served as a cook in the US Occupational Army in Germany from June 3, 1919 to May 16, 1922.

I have no idea how, why or when he came to San Diego. Sam had one brother, Isaias, who lived in Mexico where he owned several furniture stores. In September of 1945, he moved to Chula Vista with his wife, Ida, and their five children: Elena, who is my age, Moses, Ethel, Joel, and Michael. Isaias passed away at age 45.

Leah Addleson was born in London, England on March 14, 1899 and was the youngest in the family. She had four brothers and three sisters. Nathan, a rabbi, married Anna, and they had two daughters, Silvia and Essie. After Anna's death, he married Clare, a lovely English lady. Brother Moss married Esther and had Eleanor and Ernie; Jack married Frances and had one daughter, Olga; and Harry married Lena and had one daughter, Estelle. They divorced, and Harry married Ann. Her sisters were Jennie, whose husband passed away before the last of their four sons, Babe, was born. His older brothers were Harold, Henry, and Bernard.

Sam in Coblenz, Germany, 1919 with 3
Chambermaids and a cook.

Sophie married Lou Gabor, a tailor, and they had
no children; and Miriam, was married to Irving
Schneider, born in Hungary, had Ruthie and a son
Julie.*

Jennie came to the United States first, settled in
Ogden, Utah and married a man in the furniture
business.

She brought the rest of her other siblings and her

*Julie was married for several years, then divorced and
never remarried. He was my best man at our wedding
and attended our 50th anniversary party. He passed
away in 2012 at age 86.

parents to Utah before World War I and then they all moved either to Los Angeles or San Diego.

Leah came to New York on May 1, 1915 on the ship Saint Louis. Leah's uncle, Louie Addleson and his wife, Fanny, better known as Tanta, came from Russia to Utah and then to San Diego with their five boys and four girls. In the 1940-50s, San Diego was still a small town, and it seemed that most Jewish families were related to the Addlesons.

Ironically, none of the Addlesons on either side had many children, mostly just one or two, and the males all had girls, except for Leah's brother, Moss, who had one son, Ernie. Ernie and his wife, Ellen, had three girls, Elyse, Edie and Elana. One of Leah's uncle's sons, Eddie, had two daughters, Arlene and Joyce, and one son Larry, who had three sons. Eddie's brother Harry, who had one son, was the only ones to carry on the family name.

Sam had a kosher butcher shop on Market Street in San Diego when he married Leah, who was working at Strugo's, a women's accessories shop.

Sam and Leah married in Los Angeles on January 3, 1926

Leah, brother-in-law Lou Gabor, and Sam holding his son Joel

Joel and Leah Shapov

Sam's butcher shop closed shortly after he and Leah were married, and he went into the cattle business at a ranch they leased in Sunny Side, which is east of Chula Vista. Leah wasn't used to this kind of life since she didn't drive and there was no public transportation to downtown San Diego. So after a few years they moved to a ranch at 334 C Street, Chula Vista. This ranch consisted of 30 acres of river bottomland in Sweetwater Valley, San Diego County on the north side of C Street and east of Highland Avenue. They bought it for $1500 from Adolph Levi, a rancher and wealthy landowner. Their payments were $35 per month. I went with Sam several times to make the payments at Adolph's office in the old Bank of America building at Sixth and Broadway in downtown San Diego.

Sam rented an additional 10 acres from the Mosholders family on the south side of C Street that had a small old farmhouse on a hill, plus a shack and barn below.

Fast Forward:

Sam bought the 10 acres years later for $6500.

C Street was the boundary between the city of Chula Vista and San Diego County. There was a bus stop on the corner of C Street and 4th Avenue where the street going north changed to Highland Avenue, just one block west of the house, and that made Leah happy. Neither Leah nor any of her sisters ever drove, and most families owned only one automobile.

Sam and Leah had the misfortune of losing a child at birth and one as an infant. Their third child, Joel, was an avid baseball player. Sometime in late 1941, he was struck on the ankle by a hardball, and it became infected. They took him to the Mayo Clinic, but to no avail. The infection had spread throughout his body. He passed away on June 26, 1942 at the age of 12 ½.

Fast Forward:

After Leah died on December 26, 1977 at age 78, I found one of Joel's baseballs, his key chain with his initials (J S), a baseball charm, a 10 Commandments pin, and a baby picture.

After Joel's death, someone suggested that Sam and Leah bring another child into their home. Leah's brother, Nathan (Natie) Addleson was a well-known rabbi in Los Angeles. It must have been his idea that they go to Vista Del Mar to find, if possible, a candidate to fill Joel's void.

I was available and ready, but was Leah ready?

Looking back at the circumstances, I can only surmise that Leah was not ready emotionally to care for another child so soon after losing hers.

Fast Forward:

A few years ago, Norma and I happened to be in Chula Vista and decided to visit Pauline Spangler, who with her (late) husband John had operated a restaurant on the Shapov's ranch. She was delighted to see us, especially since she was in the process of packing to move that week to the Midwest where her family lived.

Sam Shapov spent a lot of time at the restaurant drinking coffee and talking with her. On one of these occasions, Pauline asked Sam how I had come to live with him and Leah. He related the story, which I had never heard before or ever would have if we had not stopped at her house that day.

Again, timing is everything in life.

Sam told her that after they dropped me off at Vista Del Mar and began driving away, I started to cry and he turned the car around and came to get me. Pauline also inquired why they never officially adopted me. He told her they thought maybe some of my family would show up, and they would somehow become responsible for them too.

The subject of adoption was never brought up, which didn't bother me since I wanted to keep my own name anyway. I think Sam, and certainly Leah, were under pressure from one of her nephews not to adopt me.

Again, for the last time, I packed my very few belongings; my photo album and pictures, my memories and moved to the ranch in Chula Vista, just south of San Diego.

Chapter 10
The Ranch, My New Home

It was a late September afternoon in 1942 after a three-hour drive south to Chula Vista with me sitting in the back seat alone when Sam turned left off Highland Avenue onto C Street. It was a bumpy dirt road with barbed-wire fences on both sides enclosing the very poor river bottom pastureland. The road came to a small hill after a distant of one city block, and we turned right into the driveway of a small wooden farmhouse with a large pepper tree and a small empty cement fishpond in front. There was a chicken coop in the back and a large playhouse on the side of the driveway, which the original owners of the property had built.

The house was all lit up, and there was a large stout woman busy cooking. It was Jennie Siner, Leah's older widowed sister. Estelle Addleson (Leah's brother Harry's daughter) was also there to welcome me, check me out, or maybe both. The house consisted of a small living room on the right as you walked in and a dining room on the left. In the middle was the door leading into the kitchen to the right and a dinette area on the left, as well as a door leading into a small bedroom that was to be mine.

The bedroom was about 8 x 10 feet with a window facing east overlooking the driveway. There was a small closet and dresser, both completely empty, a single bed with a small table that fit between the bed and the side of the closet, and a small ivory Philco radio. As small and simple as it was, it was the first time in my life, as far as I could remember, that I had my own bedroom or lived in a private home. There were absolutely no signs of any child ever having lived there. I was thrilled.

Leading from the kitchen was a hallway to the rear of the house with the master bedroom on the left and a bathroom on the right. Behind them, two steps down to a cement floor, was an enclosed back porch. It housed the water heater, ringer washing machine, a double washbasin, an extra refrigerator, and an old icebox where Leah kept candy and several large crocks to make pickles, and a storage closet. On the left side was the back entrance to the house and on the right side was the door to the clotheslines.

Fast forward:

The house was remodeled a few years later with the living room enlarged, a front porch added as well as, in the back, two bedrooms, a bath and office with an outside entrance, and a double garage.

Chapter 11-The Adjustment

At age eleven, I set out on a new phase of my life of being a member of a large family and living in a private home. I also inherited all the problems associated with being the Shapov's new child so soon after having lost their own. This was quite a challenge, which was overcome in time with a great deal of effort and patience by all. I never, even once, thought about them taking me back to Vista Del Mar.

Can a "normal" home life that begins at age eleven have a major effect on the future development of a child? Has a child developed most of his characteristics by this time or is he still young enough to have his character molded? These were some of the questions I had to struggle with subconsciously. Can you imagine trying to fill Joel's shoes? Leah used to cry a lot during the first year, which was understandable. I don't think she was ready to care or love an orphan or any other child for that matter. Was I only there to fill their void and not because they wanted to nurture an orphan? This issue didn't help my emotional needs.

Fast Forward:

At the OSE reunion in 1989 in Los Angeles, a survey was taken of the orphans who went to live in foster homes. Some had lived in as many as five different homes and some had to compete with other

*foster and or natural children. I had to compete with a
dead child I never knew. Even today, I know very little
about Joel Shapov. They never talked about Joel, which
if they had, might have been the best thing for all.*

My new home life was very simple but nice. I never
gave Sam or Leah any problems or ever made demands.
I was grateful for what I had. Leah was very nervous
and any little thing would aggravate her. I tolerated her
and never built up any resentment. I knew she was
doing her best under the circumstances. Sam's main
problem was that he was a heavy smoker.

It's ironic how one child's death brought new life to
another.

Chapter 12-Back to the Ranch

I loved exploring the ranch. As you came out of the driveway and turned right onto the dirt road (C Street which extended east to Second Avenue) and went downhill, there was a shack on the right where Mack Wallenstein, the hired help, lived. There was a shed and a cement dairy barn that was hardly ever used. To the left of the road going up a steep hill, were the cattle corrals and a wooden milking barn. Mack was a strong middle-aged man of German descent, who could build or repair almost anything as well as being very good with animals. He enjoyed his wine, and many times had a little too much.

There were cows, calves, chickens, a workhorse name Dolly, and a pig (the garbage disposal). There was also a pair of geese; one white that laid gigantic eggs that Leah used to make into deviled eggs, and a grey one named Betsy. As it turned out, Betsy was the male, and he loved Leah. He would follow her like a puppy and would peck her cheeks as if to kiss her. On one occasion, he even jumped on her head. One day he followed her all the way to the bus stop and she had to come back and put him in the coop.

I had a dog named Spotty, Spot for short, for 6 or 7 years. I raised from a puppy. His mother was a cocker spaniel and the sire was a curbside ambassador. Ha! During my years at the ranch I had several other dogs including Foxy. Spotty loved going out in the pasture with me to bring in the cows at milking time and he loved chasing cars that drove by on C Street, which resulted in a bad hind leg. We always had cats as well.

It was great living on the ranch. I started to help with the farm chores and loved working with the animals. A few months after I arrived Sam gave me a Guernsey, a brown-and-white calf that I named Rabbit because she wiggled her ears. She was my first real responsibility. I raised her until she had a calf and I then sold her to Joe Ferrari, who owned a dairy in what is now the Grantville area.

Rabbit as a calf and as a cow with her own calf

Betsy the goose and Leah looking east

Spotty -Looking west towards 4th & C Street

Werner and Spotty

Sam had Dolly bred to a stallion owned by Tom
Eaton, a dairyman at Lincoln Acres, a few miles away
from the ranch. Tom's son, Jack, and I were very good
friends. I can still remember how excited I was when on
May 5, 1944 Dolly had her foul, which we named
Tamalain or Tammy for short. She became my horse.
Leah had once read a book with a horse named
Tamalain. When Tammy was old enough, we had her
trained and I would ride her almost every day, bare
back or with a western saddle.

Jack and I would collaborate in horseshow events
and ride in the Chula Vista Fiesta Del La Luna parade.
During summer vacation, some of the kids from nearby
dairies with horses and I would ride out to Bonita, just
east of Chula Vista, where Tom's dairy had relocated.

We would meet Jack by the bridge and ride into tall
under-growth bushes next to a watermelon patch owned
by a farmer, John Esterbloom. The melons were
delicious.

Fast Forward:

*Jack enlisted in the USMC before finishing high
school and was deployed to Korea. A week prior to his
scheduled return home he was killed in action. He is
buried at Glen Abbe in Bonita overlooking a small
pond. His father was buried next to him when he
passed away. There was a plaque placed in his memory
at the fire station, now a museum, in Bonita.*

Tammy and Dolly in the 30-acre field

With Spotty, Tammy and Rabbit and all the other
animals on the ranch, I didn't miss having kids around
and only saw them at school. The closest neighbor lived
a block away. There wasn't even mail delivery on C
Street. Sam had box, #655, at the Chula Vista Post
office. The phone number was Chula Vista 197.

Me on Tammy. Cattle corrals in background

Sam milking and smoking

Sam showing cows to buyers

World War II was still going on, and meat, butter and gas were rationed. There was always a lot of fresh milk and in the summer I would drink as much as one gallon a day. After the milk sat for a day in the refrigerator, we would take the cream off the top and put it in a hand churn and make butter. We had molds to make 1-pound cubes. The buttermilk, from making the butter, always went to the pig since no one liked it. Sam would get tongue, liver and oxtails from the slaughterhouses in National City where he sold some of his cattle. Sam, given his Army experience, and Leah were both great cooks. He made the best fried chicken and Leah the best sweet-and-sour tongue, braised oxtails or soup, liver and onions as well as delicious lemon pies, fruit and honey cakes. There were several beehives on the ranch and the owner would bring us a 5-gallon can of honey whenever we ran out.

Leah also made dill pickles and tomatoes in the big crocks on the back porch.

Every Saturday morning, Leah would walk to the corner of 4th and C Streets and take the bus to downtown San Diego, meet her sister Miriam Schneider and go shopping, mainly at the Grand Rapids Department Store. Then they would take the streetcar to Miriam's house in the Burlington area, south of North Park.

In the evening, Sam and I would drive to Miriam's husband's, Irving's, Liberty Loan" pawnshop at 3rd and F in downtown San Diego, stay until closing time and drive him home. We would eat dinner at their house and then drive home to Chula Vista.

Werner, Miriam, (Leah's sister), and Irving Schneider at their Pawnshop, Liberty Loan at 3rd & F Street, San Diego 1943

Most of my clothing were hand-me-downs from their son, Julie, or the pawnshop, where I am sure my bedroom Philco radio came from.

Every Saturday, Leah would give me 60 cents to go to the Seville Theater on 3rd Avenue and G Street. I'd usually walk. The double-feature movie cost 50 cents, and included a newsreel, cartoon and a serial that ended with a cliffhanger and continued the following week. Candy and drinks were five cents each. Sometimes I would only buy candy and then on the way home buy a 5-cent ice cream cone at the Rexall Drugstore, which at times contained a coupon in the bottom for a free one. When that happened, it was big time.

One Saturday, Leah didn't have any change and gave me a $5 bill. On my way home from the movie I had some money left over and I thought it would be nice to buy her a gift from one of the stores on 3rd Avenue. I found some nice ice tongs and was so proud of making the purchase, only to have her raise hell with me for spending the money. I never bought her anything again with her money. She didn't make me return them and used them for many years. Norma and I now have them.

This surely didn't help build any confidence.

Chapter 13
Chula Vista and Grammar School

In 1942, Chula Vista was a beautiful small town surrounded by lemon orchards, just 15 miles north of Mexico with a population of approximately 5000. The main business corner was 3rd Avenue and F Street, with 3rd Avenue extending south only to D Street where it merged with Sea Valle Street heading east and overlooking the ranch to the left. There was a grass island with palm trees from F to G Street with a Safeway, Bank of America and Gilbert's Drugstore and another small bank on the corners. The public library was one block to the east on F Street. The main employer was Rohr Aircraft, which got into some sort of dispute with the city so had two armored trucks bring its entire payroll from the San Francisco Mint in silver dollars to show the effect they had on the city. Rohr made their point.

I entered F Street Grammar School at the corner of 4th and F Street in the fourth grade since I struggled in English. I must have been somewhat of a novelty, this little German kid who spoke very little English. Some of the kids would bully and tease me, which resulted in some fights and visits to the principal's office. Prior to this, I had always been a very quiet easygoing kid. However, I made many lifelong friends.

In the 6th grade, Mrs. Holmes was my teacher and she knew me since her family, as did many others during the war, owned a cow from which they got fresh milk. Once a year the families would bring their cow to the ranch to be bred for $3. This was the case for Mrs. Holmes' family. She became my mentor and really settled me down. She spent extra time with me, giving me encouragement, helping me to integrate with the other kids, teaching me to speak, read and write English. I was never in the principal's office again and started building my confidence and self-esteem.

Fast forward:

I used to visit Mrs. Holmes who lived across the street from the new Chula Vista High School at 4th and K Street where I attended. As I was plowing through old albums researching for this book, I found two certificates from the City of Chula Vista, acknowledging my service on the Junior Traffic Patrol in years 1944 and 1945, and one an Honorable Discharge Certificate, which I thought was very funny. I must have been a doer even then.

By the time I entered junior high, I was able to skip one grade and then another grade going into high school.

The nice part of growing up in a small town like Chula Vista was that most of the children from grammar school stayed together all the way through junior high and high school. In addition, you knew most of the local merchants through their kids in your classes.

Every year, Chula Vista held a Fiesta De La Luna with a parade going down Third Avenue and ending at a big carnival in the Eucalyptus Park across from the ranch. When I was about 15, I opened the fence from the pasture and created a parking lot business. Sam let me keep the money I earned.

Chapter 14-My Bar Mitzvah

Sam and Leah were members of the Orthodox Tifereth Israel Synagogue located on 18th and Market in San Diego, where most of the Jewish community lived. It was a small European, old-style, synagogue with the bima in the middle and the women sitting upstairs.

Sam and Leah enrolled me in Hebrew school to prepare me for my Bar Mitzvah. I would take the city bus every weekday after school to 12th and Market Street, then transfer to 18th and Market. The monthly bus pass cost $1.50. How times have changed! My Bar Mitzvah was on March 20, 1944, which Alice (Low-Zimmer) Feldman and her entire family attended. Afterwards we had lunch at Lou and Sophie (Leah's sister) Gabor's house across the street from the synagogue.

A few years later, Rabbi Morten Cohen from Beth Israel Temple at Fourth & Laurel formed the Temple Youth League (TYL), which was open to all the Jewish teenagers in the San Diego and surrounding area. This was great, especially for me living quite a distance away in Chula Vista. There was always some activity planned every Sunday and it was a great way to meet kids from all over the city, many of whom I am still friends with, including Zane Feldman and Edie (Press) Greenberg.

Chapter 15
Alice (Low-Zimmer) and Zane Feldman

Alice Low-Zimmer moved to San Diego on December 7, 1941, at age 10, with her family after having lived in Denver for two years. She, her parents Bernard and Sophie, and older sister, Margaret, came from Czechoslovakia where her father was in the cattle business.

Adolph Levi, the man Sam Shapov bought the 30 acres in Sweetwater Valley from, was Bernard's uncle. He came to the United States in the 1890s as a single man, settled in San Diego, went into the cattle business and bought lots of land all around the county, including Mission Valley, some of which his estate still owns. He sold Bernard a house on 18th Street, a few blocks north of the synagogue and introduced him to Sam Shapov with hopes that he would find him a job as a butcher, which he did. They became good friends and that is how I met Alice.

According to Alice, in 1935 Adolph Levi returned to Czechoslovakia to attend his sister's wedding and met a beautiful 16 year-old girl who was very well endowed physically, brought her back to San Diego and married her. They had two children, Edgar and Selma, lived in the famous El Cortez Hotel, and paid $300 per month rent, which was a lot of money in those days.

Coincidently, Louie and Ethel Feldman and their two children, Estelle and Zane, also moved to San Diego on December 7, 1941 from Los Angeles. Louie, who had retired from an insurance business, came to run his brother's donut business.

I first met Zane, who was a tall, thin, good-looking chap with thick, wavy black hair, at a Sunday TYL gathering, as did Alice. He is one year older than I.

Fast Forward:

I was an usher at their wedding on October 22, 1950. Zane was an usher at Norma's and my wedding in 1954. We have remained best friends to this day.

After Zane returned from his US Army duty, he opened a drapery and upholstery fabric store in North Park at the corner of 30th and Wightman Streets in San Diego.

Over the last 55 years, we have always lived within a mile of each other and have gone on many cruises and vacations together. In addition, we still fight at the bridge table.

Earlier in the book, I mentioned how the Addleson's (Leah's family) were related to so many. Alice and Zane's daughter Lisa married Rob Orlansky whose mother, Arlene, is the daughter of Leah's cousin Eddie Addleson. So we are kind of related.

Chapter 16
Junior High and High School, Etc.

I continued school at G Street Junior High School at 5th and G with all the kids from F Street Grammar School, as well as many students from other grammar schools, including Billy Casper*, who became a famous golfer.

I had become quite fluent in English by this time and was secretary and treasurer for my 7th grade homeroom class.

The war and rationing ended in 1945.

There was a golf driving range on the field at the northwest corner of 4th and C Street across from the ranch, where I worked part-time picking up golf balls. I saved up $25 dollars and bought a used Victory bicycle that I rode to junior high. That was the only bicycle I ever owned. I took such good care of it; I was able to sell it 3 years later for $20.

*Billy Casper passed away February 7, 2015. He was one of the most successful professional golfers.

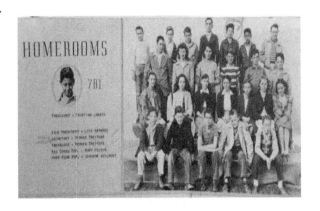

1945 7th grade, Werner, 3rd from the right, back row, secretary and treasurer of the class

I became homeroom rep in the 7th grade and Audrey Holmes, the nicest and prettiest girl in junior and senior high, was president. She was voted the best personality in senior high school, and was a cheer leader, and in many other activities. We have remained friends and she attend our out 50th wedding anniversary party.

Being a class officer must have helped my self-esteem.

8th grade class 1946 Audrey Holmes, president,
Werner homeroom rep

I didn't participate in any after-school activities
since I was getting more involved in ranch chores.

Sweetwater High School at 30th & Highland in
National City was the only high school in the area all
the way to the Mexican border, and it was
overcrowded. In 1947, the new Chula Vista High
School opened. Our principal from junior high, Joseph
Rindone, came with us and later became district
superintendent several years after I graduated.

During the two years of building the new high
school campus at 4th and K Street, we were bussed to a
temporary location at Brown Field at Otay Mesa near
the Mexican border until the new campus was ready. It
had been an Air Force base during the war.

Like many boys, I didn't have much interest in high school and used to live for the day I would graduate. I didn't think I would be able to afford college. Then I started taking agriculture classes, got involved in Future Farmers of America (FFA), and in a short time became president of the school chapter. This again was a great step in helping me overcome my subconscious inferiority complex.

My agriculture teacher, Robert Mills, was a Cal Poly graduate and got me interested in going to college. With the war raging in Korea, I had no desire to go there. College would exempt me for four years if my grades were good. During my last years in high school I really started studying and got all A's.

I raised several steers, Lucky and Nuisance, as my FFA project and showed them at the San Diego County Fair at Del Mar, as well as the Mid-Winter Fair in Imperial Valley. I won second-place prizes for each steer as well as a showmanship award.

I sold them at the San Diego Del Mar Fair auction, where the price was always much higher than on the regular market. That helped with college tuition at California State Polytechnic at San Luis Obispo.

I also won a small scholarship from Sears Roebuck.

Trophy and Ribbons won by Werner Dreifuss
1949-50

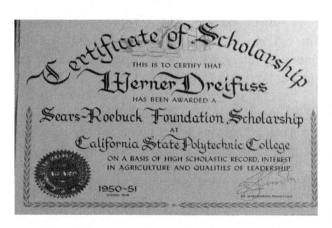

This award came with a $100 scholarship

Top: Werner Dreifuss before at the ranch and after at
the 1950 Del Mar Fair with steers "Lucky.
   Bottom L: Del Mar Fair queen, Nuisance and I.
   R; Nuisance and me

One of my best high school friends was Sammy Wolfsdorf who was born in Mexico and lived with his mother in San Ysidro. He excelled in all sports especially football. He was co-captain of the Chula Vista High School football team. Sammy attempted to enlist in the military after graduation, but was rejected. However, shortly afterwards he was drafted, sent to Korea and was killed in action on August 31, 1951 just one week after arriving there. He was buried at Greenwood Home of Peace Cemetery, San Diego, in the same area as Joel, Sam and Leah Shapov. Chula Vista named a street in his honor. Sammy was one of only seven Jewish students at Chula Vista High School. Rest in peace my friend.

Sammy Wolfsdorf display at Chula Vista High School.

In my senior year in high school, I had asked a very nice girl whom I knew from TYL and that I loved to dance with to my senior prom and she gladly accepted. Several days before the dance, she called crying to tell me her father wouldn't let her go with me. They were a well to do family in San Diego. I wasn't good enough for his daughter. Several years later, her father went to jail for tax evasion and that got him off his high horse.

I got another date to the prom.

Werner's Wisdom:

Tommy Thompson was a wealthy man and part owner of a dairy cattle sale yard in El Monte, California where we would buy cows from for resale in the San Diego area. He would come to the ranch quite often and always drove a nice car. On one occasions, he arrived in a different car. I asked him what had happened to the previous one. He said he sold it and I asked why. He replied, "Never marry anything but a wife; everything else sell if you can make a good profit." I never forgot that.

Sam bought several cars from him, some of which he gave me including a grey 2-door coup 1948 Chrysler Highlander that had a beautiful plaid interior and an interior button for the gas cap release, which at that time was a luxury. I named it the grey ghost.

I was always thankful throughout the years of living on the ranch, and yet, for some reason felt I carried more than my own weight by doing chores without ever being told or asked to and helping buy and sell cattle. I never made any demands.

On March 5, 1953, I was so proud to become a US citizen. Leah came with me to the swearing-in ceremony at the courthouse in San Diego.

March 5th also happens to be our youngest grandson Sammy's birthday. So it's always a double celebration.

There are two poems that that were taught in my last year in grammar school that have always been in my mind and part of my life.

The first is Rudyard Kipling's "If" with the last lines, "If you can walk with kings or common man and not lose your virtue, you are a man, my son."

The second is Joyce Kilmer's "Trees" with the last line, "But only God can make a tree."

Chapter 17
Otay Mesa and Ranch Property

During 1946-1948, Sam leased 700 acres of pasture on Otay Mesa from Harry Lampki, a frugal bachelor of German descent, whose parents had homesteaded there. During droughts they kept buying land at very low prices. We would keep young heifers there, and Harry would move them from one 40-acre section to another as the water holes dried up and/or the grass became scarce.

In early 1949, Harry offered to sell the land to Sam for $37.50 per acre, which at that time was a lot of money that he didn't have. So Sam got Robert Egger, a well-to-do dairyman and vegetable farmer from Palm City, to come in as a partner. A short time after buying the property, Robert wanted to spend a lot of money to drill water wells and start farming, and offered to buy Sam out. He agreed to pay $5000 in principle and $5000 in interest each year. I don't remember what the total price was, but it would be the first time in Sam's life, other than the Army, that he would have a steady income and be able to travel, and I advised him to sell it. Within a year after selling the property, Harry died. I bought my first car, a 1929 Model a Ford 4-door sedan, a 2-cow trailer and an old tractor with big steel wheels that ran on kerosene and had to be hand cranked to

start, from his estate for $200. I sold the trailer for
$150. I was so proud of the car.

Werner and Foxy with her puppies.
Picture taken a few years before I bought this
Model A from the Lampki estate.

Fast forward:

*The year Sam and Leah sold the Otay Mesa
property, they and her brother, Moss Addleson, and his
wife Esther (Ernie's parents) went to Canada on a
vacation. They bought a fancy bottle of Crown Royal
whiskey in a blue velvet bag, drank about half and
brought the rest home. Since then, they have all passed
away. In 1979 on our first luxury cruise with Ernie and
Ellen to Alaska, we finished the bottle in their memory.
These same bottles are still sold which goes to say, if it
isn't broken, don't fix it.*

That year, Sam bought his first and only new car, a 1948 Plymouth 4-door sedan from McCuen Plymouth - Chrysler in National City, north of Chula Vista.

Leah, Werner & Spotty   Sam, Werner and
                               1948 Plymouth

The city of Chula Vista began to grow in the late 1940's and needed to extend the main street, Third Ave. for 1 mile in order to connect with 4th St. and Highland Ave. That involved a slant cut through Sam's ten-acre property on the south side of C Street. The city of Chula Vista purchased this piece of property, which created commercial land on both sides of the 3rd Ave. extension.

A motor vehicle office was built on the east side of the 3rd Avenue extension below the ranch house. The restaurant John and Pauline Spangler leased was on the southeast corner of 4th and C Street. The dirt excavated from the motor vehicle office site was used to fill the

front part of the 30 acres on Highland Avenue, which was river bottom. It was annexed to the city of Chula Vista and eventually sold for commercial development.
Fast Forward:

Sixty-six years later, threads connect. While waiting for the evening show in the Crystal Cove during our 2014 World Cruise, there was a couple sitting next to us. Norma introduced us and told them we were from San Diego. The lady looks at me, and much to my surprise, says," You're the orphan." I said "Yes, but how did you know?" She said that Tommy* had told her my story since they were from San Diego. She introduced herself as Nancy and her husband Tony McCuen. I said "From McCuen Motors, honest?" He owned a car dealership in National City, just north of Chula Vista and always ended his TV commercial with "honest." We quoted him many times in our store. He also had a dog in his TV commercials named Spot like my dog. They were celebrating their first anniversary since selling the agency.

Sam had bought his first and only new car, a 1948 Plymouth from Tony's father. Tony joined his father in the business that same year.

*We met Tommy Schweiger and his wife Heather on our first World Cruise in 2009 and again on other Crystal cruises and have become good friends. He was also born in Germany and immigrated to England with his parents in 1938 at the age of one. They live in

Manchester, United Kingdom. He is a happy, slightly loud, short, stout sort of chap and always refers to me as his Pa-Pa, even though I am only 7 years older.

Me, Norma, Heather and Tommy on the 2016 Crystal World Cruise.

Chapter 18-Cal Poly

In 1950, California State Polytechnic, (Cal Poly), in Luis Obispo, California was an all-male school of about 5000 students. The most common majors were agriculture and architecture. I enrolled in the fall of 1950 as a technical student in dairy husbandry, which the college had recommended. After one and a half years, I changed to a degree program and took maximum load of 20 units each quarter in order to graduate in four years.

The first thing I did was to get a job at the campus dairy. Early in the morning, before school started I hauled milk in 10-gallon cans to their on campus creamery. During the years, I held various other jobs on campus which entitled me to a free dorm room, which was in a bungalow that had six bedrooms, bunk beds and was located near the school dairy. My roommate was Hugh Au, a tall good-natured Chinese kid from Imperial Valley. The total college cost per quarter was from $600 - $650, including everything. Try that today. I also worked at dairies around San Luis Obispo.

I became active in the Los Lecherous Dairy Club where I held most offices, as well as being selected to be a member of the Cal Poly dairy cattle judging team.

Dairy cattle judging is very similar to judging a beauty contest for women, except you have cows instead. There are five major breeds; Holsteins (white and black), Guernsey's (white and brown), Jerseys (brown), Brown Swiss' (brown but larger than Jerseys), and Ayrshires (white and red or black and white). There are four cows of the same breed and age in a group and, as a judge, your responsibly is to place them order of first, second, third and fourth. This needs to be done in a prescribed amount of time, while notes are taken as to why you placed them in such an order. Then, you go before an official judge, one for each breed, for a specified time to give him or her the reasons you placed the cows as you did. It may or may not be the same as the judge placed them, however, they will grade you on the validity and presentation of your reasons, then give you a score. You also receive a score on how well you placed the cows compared to the official judges' placing. There are three members on a dairy cattle judging team, and are scored both as a team and as individuals.

In my first year at Cal Poly, I placed second in an All-College Dairy Judging Contest, which is when I set a standard for myself that I didn't dare let down. I continued to work harder at judging to maintain the reputation I had established.

As a sophomore, I made the all-senior judging team as an alternate to the Pacific International Dairy Cattle Exposition in Portland, Oregon, where our team scored high in most divisions.

The following year I returned as a team member to win third place as an individual in the entire contest.

We drove up to Portland both years with Russell Nelson, our coach and professor from the dairy dept. At one of our spots we encounter the train General Dwight Eisenhower was campaigning from for the presidential office, which he won in 1952.

Ike campaigning

During my senior year, I was a member of the Senior Cal Poly Dairy Cattle judging team that went to the National Intercollegiate Dairy judging contest at the National Dairy Cattle Congress show at Waterloo, Iowa. This is the Super Bowl or World Series of dairy cattle judging.

There were 33 teams, 99 contestants from all major agriculture colleges throughout the United States, and I placed second in the entire contest. It marked the first time an entry west of the Mississippi ever placed in the competition.

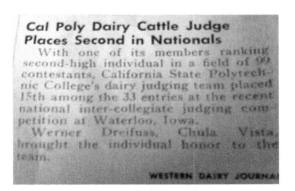

Cal Poly Dairy Cattle Judge Places Second in Nationals

With one of its members ranking second-high individual in a field of 99 contestants, California State Polytechnic College's dairy judging team placed 15th among the 33 entries at the recent national inter-collegiate judging competition at Waterloo, Iowa.

Werner Dreifuss, Chula Vista, brought the individual honor to the team.

WESTERN DAIRY JOURNAL

I'm sure I was the only foreign born and Jewish contestant. It makes me shudder just to think about it some 60 years later.

This resulted in receiving job offers from several large agricultural companies, which were declined. I knew I would be drafted soon after graduation, getting married and didn't wish to make any commitments at that time.

What was my motivation and drive? Was I determined to prove to the world that I was as good as or better than the rest? This underlying motivation has continued on throughout my life

I received every senior award possible from the dairy department during 1954.

Werner receiving the Golden State Award for
Advanced Dairy Cattle Judging

The George M. Drumm award for the outstanding
senior in the dairy department was awarded to me, and
my name was engraved on the perpetual George M.
Drumm trophy that remains at Cal Poly

George Drumm was head of the dairy department
for many years, instructor and coach of the senior
judging team, as well as developing one of the finest
dairy cattle herds in the nation.

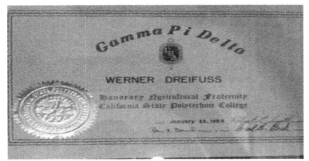
Honorary Agricultural Fraternity

Werner Dreifuss back second from the right next to
Coach Sheldon Harden

In my senior year I was on the Cal Poly wrestling
team at the 157 lb. weight.

Norma and Leah came to my graduation by train in
the middle of June 1954 when I received my bachelor's
degree in dairy husbandry.

Chapter 19-The Courtship

This chapter was originally two, the courtship according to Norma and the courtship according to me. Joe Kita's, the Memoir writing instructor on the Crystal World Cruise, recommended we combine them. It was read at the memoir readings gathering on the 2014 World Cruise. Sara Hayes, an Entertainer, read as if she was Norma and John Holly, Special Event Coordinator, as if he was me. Joe Kita and his wife Maria read it again in 2015 as a love story for Valentina's day. It was very well received both times and each was recorded on my iPad, first by the professional Dena Sterr* and the second time by me.

"**Werner**"

During summer vacation from Cal Poly in 1953, I received a call from longtime friend Edie (Press) Greenberg, who I had met at a Temple Youth League gathering. She was attending UCLA and living in Hershey Hall on campus. There she met and became friends with this nice looking (and very quiet) girl, Norma Simons, who she thought I should meet.

Norma's parents lived in Los Angeles and had recently moved to Coronado, where her mother had a baby shop, Paula's Porch Shop, at the Hotel Del Coronado. Norma came home from LA for the summer.

One evening, Edie called to tell me that Norma was at a USO dance at Temple Beth Israel. She described what Norma was wearing and suggested I go to meet her. Not being short of girlfriends I told her that I was agreeable to meeting her since one more couldn't hurt. So having nothing better to do, I went to check out the merchandise. We met and after several dances, and some talking, I told her I would call her to make a date.

Her attributes included being about five feet six inches tall, having beautiful long brown hair, a big smile, a very nice figure, a lovely personality, and being a good dancer.

On our first date I took her to Starlight Opera, an open-air theater in Balboa Park. We saw *South Pacific* in hopes of making this a very romantic evening. Afterwards I took her to the El Cortez Hotel, the finest hotel in San Diego. It had an outside glass elevator from which one could view the entire city. We had a drink and we danced. There was only one problem; she smoked a cigarette, which really turned me off. I think she was trying to impress me. Afterwards, I took her home to Coronado via a ferry since there was no bridge at that time, I never called her again. I was not interested in getting involved with anyone at the time.

"Norma" *from her scrapbook

While in my senior year and living in Hershey Hall at UCLA, I met Edie Press from San Diego. She told me of a wonderful guy she would like to fix me up with in San Diego. At that time my folks were living in Coronado where my mother had a baby shop in the Hotel Del Coronado. While I was home for the summer

Edie gave Werner my phone number. He contacted me but I was unable to go out with him the first time he asked.

Several weeks elapsed, and I did not hear from Werner. Wednesday evening August 12, 1953, he phoned and I was not home. He must have called Edie who then called my mother who told her I went to a USO dance on the temple at 3rd and Laurel Street. My mother gave a description of what I was wearing. Edie called Werner with the details. He came the USO dance. We talked, danced for a while and he asked me out for the upcoming Friday night.

We went to the Starlight Opera in Balboa Park, then for a drink and dancing in the Pacifica Room at the El Cortez Hotel, the best in San Diego. On the way home, we stopped at Oscar's drive-in to eat and I smoked a cigarette. It was clear this really turned Werner off. Many months passed before I saw or heard from him again.

"Werner"

In October, while in my senior year at Cal Poly, I received a letter, or should I say an invitation, from Edie, the matchmaker, telling me that she and Norma had transferred to San Diego State College. Norma was president of her sorority and in need of a date for a Thanksgiving dinner they were having. Well, not being one to pass up a free meal, I accepted.

DRINKING IN THE SKY . . . a never-to-be forgotten view · EL CORTEZ SKY ROOM, San Diego, California

Sky room 1953 at the El Cortez Hotel

When I arrived at the sorority house on Montezuma Road, the girls quickly put an apron on me and had me carve the turkey. I figured that is why they had invited me. I knew all the girls there and realized it was a MRS Sorority for desperate young Jewish girls looking for husbands. I must admit it was a very enjoyable evening.

I felt obligated to reciprocate since Norma was the "president" so I took her out for dinner Friday night and then again on Saturday night. On Sunday, I drove back to Cal Poly, which was about a 7 ½ to 8-hour drive.

The next thing I knew, Norma was sending me letters, and boxes of cookies every day with Alka-

Seltzer in case I got sick from them. I think I must have answered some of the letters to say thank you.

When I came home for Christmas vacation I happened to stop by Moss's, and his wife Esther's pawnshop, Western Jewelry and Loan. Esther looked and me and said, "I hear you're engaged." I replied, "To whom?" However, it was too late and in order to save Norma's reputation and honor, I had no choice but to go along with the story.

To make some money over the holidays, I teamed up with a friend of mine who had a connection with a Christmas tree wholesaler and we went into Christmas tree business on the ranch property in Chula Vista. Norma and I began seeing one another every day since she and my friend's girlfriend would come to the Christmas tree lot every afternoon to "help" and stay there until we closed. To tell the truth, they were a big help and we didn't have to pay them

"Norma"

It was close to Thanksgiving in 1953 when the sorority, where I was now president, was having a Thanksgiving dinner. Edie and some of the other girls decided I should ask Werner to be my date. Edie phoned Mrs. Shapov who informed her that Werner would be home for Thanksgiving. Edie was all smiles and quickly wrote Werner and asked him if he would be my date at the sorority's Thanksgiving dinner. He gladly accepted the invitation. We had a wonderful time and went out every night that weekend until it was time again for Werner to travel back to San Luis Obisbo.

He returned again to San Diego from school for Christmas vacation on December 9, 1953. We began seeing each other every day at the Christmas tree lot. Working there was a definite benefit.

For New Year's Eve, we went to the Fireside Inn in Escondido with several other couples. That evening was the first time he told me he loved me. I asked him if he was kidding or drunk. I later confessed I loved him too.

January 10, 1954 Edie and Dean Greenberg got married. Per Werner's suggestion, Edie throw her bridal bouquet towards me and I caught. It was quite embarrassing when people walked up and started congratulating Werner and me when there were not any congratulations in order.

After Edie and Dean's wedding, Werner drove back to school. He wrote every single day. When he came home again, I never in my life was so happy to see someone.

On Saturday evening, February 20, 1954, my family had dinner with Werner and his family. After dinner, in Werner's room, he popped the BIG question and at 9:35 p.m. presented me with his fraternity pin.

Saturday evening, or better yet, Sunday morning, 2 am March 21, 1954 he slipped an engagement ring onto my finger.

"Werner"

Norma was a bridesmaid at Edie (Press) and Dean Greenberg's wedding. During the reception when Edie tossed out her bridal bouquet to the eligible ladies, Norma threw a body block into the girls and caught the bouquet. People started coming up to congratulate us.

After we were engaged, we drove to Culver City to visit Norma's favorite cousin, Hal Mishkin and his wife Barbara. Norma slept with Barbara and I with Hal. How times have changed.

Norma was scheduled to meet me at a predetermined time to obtain our wedding licenses, which cost all of $2. She had agreed to pay half. First, she was late to the appointment, and then she told me she had just been shopping, and "had no money." This is still her favorite line. She has yet to pay" her half, and she definitely learn to use credit cards.

While preparing for this book, I came across a small pocket size calendar book with a notation on June 27, 1954, "My wedding don't forget".

I didn't.

Chapter 20-Norma and Family

Norma was born in Lyingin Hospital in Chicago, Illinois on August 22, 1933, (with a golden spoon in her mouth) weighing 6 lb. 3 oz. Her mother, Pearl Dorothy (Harris) Simons, was born in London, and her father, Martin Simons, was born in Chicago. Paula was a schoolteacher until she married in January 1925. Martin served in the US Army during WW1, was shot near his heart and a silver plate was placed in his chest. A dictionary in his shirt pocket deflected the bullet from his penetrating his heart.

Two siblings followed, Carol Joy (now Caryl) born January 23, 1936 and Herbert Myron born April 11, 1941.

The family was orthodox and quite well to do. Martin owned several luggage and shoe repair shops.

The dictionary that saved Martin's life

In 1945, Paula's sister, Ann Mishkin, moved from Chicago to Los Angeles with her husband, Josh, and their three sons: David, Hal (Norma's favorite cousin), and Charles, better known as "Sheppy."

Six months later, Paula and the children moved to Culver City, California, while Martin stayed in Chicago to liquidate their business. Paula and Ann started buying property, which turned out to be worthless. Their privileged lives they had enjoyed in Chicago were rapidly changing. Norma's parents never anticipated the struggles they would endure after having invested in worthless property and with Martin receiving money only from his disability payments. During the war, rationing was imposed and the family was no longer able to keep kosher. Fortunately, Norma, her sister and brother had protected college funds set up when they were born. Norma graduated from Hamilton High School in Los Angeles in 1951 and went on to UCLA (she always dreamed of becoming a dress designer – the likes of the famous Edith Head).

Paula had two brothers, Max, who was 20 years older, and Michael, who was younger. Max and wife, Minnie, had two sons: Allan, a doctor, and Sammy, a lawyer. Martin, her father, had five brothers and one older sister, Charlotte, who became a nun after their parents died.

Fast forward:

Approximately 53 years ago, Rose, (from Chicago) the wife of one of Norma's late cousin's informed us that Aunt Charlotte (her father's sister) had died in San Francisco and left an estate consisting of a small portfolio of stocks along with 40 acres of land, including the mineral rights in Dewey County, Oklahoma. We have no knowledge as to how she acquired the stocks or land but can only surmise that it happened before she became a nun and moved to San Francisco. Her estate was left to many of her living relatives, including Norma, Sister Carol, and brother Herb.

Norma's cousin Hy, also an heir, her brother Herb, our son Joel, who was six years old, and I drove to Oklahoma to check out the land and attend the sale. In order to pay the taxes, attorney fees, etc. the portfolio and the land were sold but not the mineral rights. Over the last 52 years, Norma has been leasing the mineral rights. Several years ago, a gas well was completed and Norma has been getting a monthly check of about $100.

Uncle Izzy was Martin's oldest brother. He had five children, but Norma has no information on the family. One brother, Harold Simons, lived in Los Angeles with his wife Frieda. They had three daughters, Ruth, the oldest, who never married, worked for the Lane Bryant Company for many years and later owned several women's dress shops in Arizona where she is currently living. Their second daughter, Gloria, also lived in Arizona, was married, and had two children. She passed away several years ago as did the youngest daughter, Myrna, who had lived in Los Angeles and had three children. Her husband Dan, passed away many years ago. Another brother, Jake and his wife, Fanny lived in Boil Heights, Los Angeles and had two children, Hy and Ruth.

Hy, who Norma was always very close to, and his wife Lil had five sons; Norman, married to Sandy, Fred, Sherwin, Jack, and Barney, our ring bearer, who was born when Lil was 52 years old. Jack and Barney have passed away.

Sometime in the early 1950s, the name Simons became Simmons and Pearl became Paula. Norma was 17 and decided to keep her name as Simons.

Norma's Uncle Dave stayed in Chicago and had two sons, Robert, (Rose's husband), and Herman. Hy, Robert, Rose and Norma always maintained a close relationship.

Chapter 21
The Engagement and Wedding

Norma and I celebrated our engagement as well as Herbie's Bar Mitzvah in April 1954 in Norma's parents' backyard in Coronado. Norma's family and friends came from Los Angeles as did many of Sam and Leah's family members.

Caryl Joy, Paula, Herb, Martin, Norma and me at engagement and Bar Mitzvah party in Coronado 1954

Norma set our wedding date for June 27, 1954, which was one week after my graduation from Cal Poly. This particular date was chosen as after our wedding I was expecting to be drafted into the military. Eight months later this became a reality.

Norma and the families made all the arrangements for the big day. My job was to show up!

Norma borrowed Elena Shapov's (Sam's niece) beautiful wedding dress and we were married at Tifereth Israel Synagogue, at 30th and Howard in North Park, the same congregation where, in 1944, I became a Bar Mitzvah at the prior location on 18th and Island street.

In 1948 when the congregation moved from their old building they chose to affiliate with the conservative movement and became the first congregation on the west coast to do so. Rabbi Monroe Leven's from Detroit became our spiritual leader.

Rabbi Monroe Levens and Rabbi Nathan "Natie" Addleson, Leah's brother from Los Angeles, officiated at our wedding on Sunday afternoon with about 250 guests in attendance. Julie Schneider, Leah's nephew and my best man, loaned me his new Buick for the getaway.

Werner and Norma Dreifuss wedding June 27, 1954

Top row: l-r Sam & Leah Shapov**, Werner, Norma, Martin & Paula Simmons**, Herb*, Norma's brother, Jr. Usher.

Second row: Irene Schatz**, Norma's lifelong best friend and matron of honor, Julius Schneider*, **, Leah's nephew, my best man, David Mishkin, Norma's cousin, usher, Sally Weiner***, Norma's friend, bridesmaid, Ethel Shapov*, Elena's* sister, bridesmaid, Verl Lobb*, high school friend, usher, Zane Feldman* lifelong friend, usher. Ernie Addleson* lifelong friend and cousin, usher.

Front row: Clair Goodman*, Norma's second cousin from New Jersey, bridesmaid, Carole Rae Simons*, Norma's second cousin, flower girl, came from Chicago with her widowed mother Rose. Iris Leeds, bridesmaid and Caryl Joy Simmons*, Norma's sister and maid of honor.

Missing from picture is our ring bearer, Norma's second cousin Barney Simons, one of Lil's 5 sons, and Norma's cousin, Herman "Hy" Simons. He passed away some years ago.

The wedding reception and dinner was in the Mississippi Room at the Imig Manor Hotel on El Cajon Blvd. in San Diego, now the Lafayette Hotel. It was the newest hotel in San Diego at that time and very close to the synagogue.

*Attended our 50th anniversary party at the Westgate Hotel June 27, 2004.

** Passed away.

*** Killed in an auto accident in 1959.

Chapter 22-The Honeymoon

The next day we attended the San Diego County Del Mar Fair and continued on to Las Vegas where we stayed at the Moroccan Hotel on the Strip for three days. It was our first time for either of us in Las Vegas, saw some shows, enjoyed the city, and took a tour though the inside of Hoover Dam, which was very interesting.

Norma and Werner on Hoover Dam 1954 honeymoon

Note of interest:
Several years ago, there was a television documentary about how long all structures and landmarks would last if there were no humans left on earth. It was estimated that Hoover Dam would be one of the last structures to disintegrate.

We continued on to Lake Arrowhead in the San Bernardino Mountains and stayed for three more days. Back then it was a very charming little village. Norma had gone there many times when she lived in Los Angeles. We enjoyed blueberry pancakes for the first time and enjoyed some relaxation.

Norma and Werner at Lake Arrowhead 1954 honeymoon

Fast Forward:

We returned to Lake Arrowhead many times with our children. I used to refer to it as" the closest place to heaven" until they replaced the village with a modern shopping mall and lost all of its charm.

Chapter 23-Our First Home

We rented a one-bedroom furnished unit in a nice little 6-bungalow court on Division Street in National City, owned by a lovely older Italian couple, the Billelous's.

One day Norma, the newlywed, was using a hand meat-grinder, a wedding gift, and came very close to adding her fingers to the mix. The property owner heard her scream and came to bandage her finger. The first time Norma used the common washing machine with a wringer on top, her hand and arm got caught in the wringer and the property owner, again, came to her rescue.

At least once a week we played poker with our friends Alice and Zane Feldman. Esther and Arnold Belinsky who were also in our group. Esther had lived in Chula Vista and attended high school with me. Arnold was from Detroit and was in the US Navy, stationed in Coronado when they met.

Norma was working a secretarial job at the Bank of America in Chula Vista when, as expected, I received greetings from Uncle Sam requesting my services to protect our country. I didn't know Korea was our country. I reported for duty on February 16, 1955. Norma moved back in with her parents in Coronado and got a job at a real estate office.

Chapter 24
♫ This is the Army, Mr. D ♫*

My first 8 weeks of basic training were at Fort Carson, Colorado, with the eighth army infantry, Arrow 8. Ironically, this was the same Arrow 8 Sam Shapov had served in during WWI. The design of Arrow 8 unit patch is where Sam got his idea for his cattle brand; changing only the direction of the arrow to go from side to side across the middle of the eight.

On Friday nights we would have a "GI party" when we would clean our barracks and prepare for inspection on Saturday.

During one Saturday inspection, we all were standing at attention at the end of our bunks next to our cleaned and polished military displayed footlockers when a short stocky "90-day wonder" walked in. This is how we referred to 1st Lieutenants who came fresh out of college and received their ranks.

*"This is the Army Mr. Jones" was written by Irving Berlin who lived to be 101, and made famous by singer Eddie Cantor, both nice Jewish boys.

With his leather riding quirt he jumped as high as he could and banged on the side of the heating duct. Dust came flying out of all the vents. Needless to say, we had another "GI party."

When we went on a bivouac, a long march, carrying a full backpack, I quickly learned to be in front and set the pace rather than follow. We set up camp and stayed for several days in a two-man tent. We trained using and maintaining our M16 rifles and other military equipment while marching at the same time.

Our bunk beds in the barracks were more comfortable and in a much better environment than those in the bottom of the Mouzinho coming from Europe to America in June 1941.

While on duty Norma wrote to tell me her sister, Caryl Joy, and her boyfriend, Bob Goldstone, were planning to get married. Bob was from a wealthy family in Oakland, in the Navy, and stationed in Coronado.

I suggested they have their wedding during my two-week leave, rather than on the date set for several weeks later, as I was scheduled to show up at my second 8-week basic training in Hopewell, Virginia. However, they were unable to work it out.

Top: Werner during bivouac and on left firing a
machine gun and Arrow 8 patch

Norma told Carol she couldn't make a commitment
to be in their wedding party until I returned home.

Norma checked the airlines and there were three
flight changes just to get to San Diego. It would also
cost a lot of money, which we did not have.

When arriving home from the first eight weeks of
training, Norma met me in Los Angeles where her folks
were visiting her aunt and uncle, Anne and Josh

119

Mishkin, and we went there for lunch. After lunch, we were having tea when Norma's mother Paula, who was all too familiar with being the boss in her family, brought up the subject of Caryl Joy's wedding. She let me know that Norma was expected to be there. I banged my fist on the table; all the cups jumped up and I said, "Never ever tell me what to do! If Norma can make it, she will." Paula never again tried to tell us what to do. From then on we got along very well. In fact, I took very good care of her for many years.

The next day we drove to the ranch in Chula Vista where we stayed for one week. We decided to drive together to Fort Lee, Virginia, as a second honeymoon. We packed up the "Grey Ghost," a dark grey, straight-8 cylinder 1948 Chrysler Highland 2-door coup with a beautiful plaid interior and started our drive through the south, using our trusted AAA maps.

Our first stop was at the Carlsbad Caverns in New Mexico, which were spectacular. While going through Texas, we cashed in my bus ticket from the Army and tasted grits for the first time.

In Dallas, we had a flat tire, which the AAA took care of. That was the only car problem we encountered with the "Grey Ghost,"

We continued on to Atlanta and stayed for several days with my friend from Europe, Jack Hirsch (No. 4 on the manifest list), and his wife, Gladys. I had not seen Jack since we arrived in New York 14 years prior.

Jack had become a prominent well-known and respected CPA. It was great seeing him. He and Glady's showed us all the points of interest in the city.

Fast Forward:

We stayed in touch and would see each other when they came to visit Jack's sister, Flora, who lived in Corona, California and at the OSE reunion in Los Angeles in 1979.

Werner, Norma, Gladys and Jack Hirsch on their visit to California

On many of our cruises, the people we met from Atlanta always knew Jack. On one such occasion, while playing bridge, an elderly lady sat at our table, introduced herself and said she was from Atlanta. I asked, "Do you know Jack and Gladys Hirsch?" To which she replied, "I raised him and his

brother!" Jack passed away a few years ago but we still keep contact with Gladys.

From Atlanta, we continued to Hopewell and Fort Lee. We stayed on the base for several days while searching for an apartment. Hopewell was a town that time forgot. It appeared as if there hadn't been any construction done since before the Civil War. Any type of housing, was extremely scarce.

We finally found an apartment above a grocery store. There were three apartments that had been converted from one large home which the owners of the store had originally lived in. It was the best of the worst. The landlady, who was very nice, bought us a new mattress set and for eight weeks we made due.

During the day Norma would visit with the landlady in the grocery store and they became friends. She would take Norma to her beautiful home and make lunch. On weekends we would go to New Jersey or New York to sightsee and visit Norma's relatives. During this time, Norma's sister, Caryl Joy and Bob Goldstone got married. Norma did not attend the wedding.

Fast forward:

Caryl Joy and Bob had one son, Michael. Sadly, three years later they divorced.

Quartermaster School was a lot easier than the first eight weeks of basic training. I earned a certificate for a Supply Records Course which had a MOS, Military

Occupational Specialty, number of 716. Before completion of the course, I received orders for my next assignment, which was back to Fort Carson, Colorado. Group transportation was provided, the only exemption being if your wife was pregnant, permission was given to travel with her.

Our landlady took Norma straight to her family doctor. Although she hadn't, Norma said she missed her period and the doctor gave her a note stating she was pregnant. That worked and we packed up the "Grey Ghost" in the middle of July 1955 and headed to Colorado Springs via Chicago, Norma's birthplace and where she still had many relatives.

Fast forward:

In 2005, some 50 years later, we were in Richmond,Virginia, for Ernie and Ellen Addleson's grandchildren's B'nai Mitzvahs and took a drive to visit Hopewell. The grocery store was still there, with the daughter operating it. Everything looked exactly the same. She told us her mother was in a retirement home. One of the old apartments was being used as an office and the other for storage. We went upstairs and the original appliances and fixtures were still there.

Norma's first cousin, on her father's side, Bob, whom she was very close with, and his wife, Rose, lived in Los Angeles where he was an engineer for Lucite Plastic Company. He died of lung cancer at the age of 37. He never smoked.They believe it was from the plastics. After his death, Rose moved back to Chicago, where her family lived, with her two children, Carole Rae, who was our flower girl and attended our 50th anniversary party, and David.

We also spent time with her Uncle Max, Norma's mother's older brother and his wife, Minnie, as well as their two grown sons, Micky, a doctor ,and Sammy, a lawyer, and their children.

<u>Chapter 25-Return to Fort Carson</u>

We arrived in Colorado Springs and again went apartment hunting for something we could afford on our Army pay budget. We found a new 2-story building at the foot of Pikes Peak on West Vermihjo Street. There were four units upstairs and three downstairs, two in front and one in the middle facing the side parking area. The middle one was the only one available, and we took it. It had one large room and a bathroom. Behind this unit was a production plant making shoe-string potatoes. After several months, we were able to move upstairs to the front left apartment. We had two big rooms and we were across the hall from Lee (Lemo as I called him), and Ellen Modjeska. They taught us how to play bridge.

Door on the far left was our 1st apartment and the left front upstairs 2-windows, our second apartment

All tenants, many with one child, were stationed at Fort Carson.

The day before I was to report for duty, I went to Fort Carson to check it out and stopped at the 40th Field Artillery Group Headquarters to show the sergeant at the front desk my orders. Sergeant Hofer, who was in charge, advised me that the battalion I had been assigned to, the 40th Field Artillery, was in Wisconsin for summer training of National Guards and there was no need for me to join them. He asked if I could type, and seeing there was an empty desk, I replied, "Of course." "OK," he said. "I'll cut you new orders and assign you here to the 40th Field Artillery Group Headquarters. Report for duty after you settle into your apartment."

Back row R-L: Sergeant Hofer, Lee Modjeska, Stanley Hoffmem, Werner Dreifuss and others from our office

Sergeant Hofer, a portly career soldier who was not the gung-ho type, became a good friend. Lemo, as I referred to Lee, and I ran the office. Sergeant Hofer really appreciated what we did. He would give us 3-day passes and allow us to cut orders waiving the time requirements to get promotions, which meant more pay. When allocations came from post headquarters, we would distribute them to our battalions.

On September 22, 1955, I was promoted to Private First Class and to SP3 on February 16, 1956.

Requisitions also came from Post Headquarters for overseas duty assignments in Korea, as per MOS, (Military Occupational Specialty). My MOS was 716, Supply Specialist, for which there were no requests, but there were requests for MOS 711, office personnel. To avoid going to Korea, I continued with a supply MOS until my remaining time left in the army was too short to go overseas. Then we cut orders changing my MOS to 711.

Norma got a civil service job at the base Quartermaster as a secretary for a colonel and worked until our son, Joel, was born. She earned more money than I did. Norma made all her maternity clothing.

While at Fort Carson, Norma had her birthday on Monday, August 22. I bought her a card saying, "Happy Birthday to my first wife. That should keep you on your toes." (It must have worked because she is still my first wife.) There was just one problem: I had hidden the card under the car seat and for some reason thought that August 22 was on Tuesday instead of Monday. I gave her the card one day late. She was rather upset with me, but not for long.

While living in Fort Carson, Norma's younger brother, Herbie, came for a visit via Greyhound bus. He was about 14 years old and was very fussy about how and what was on his dinner plate. He wanted every item on a different plate like his mommy did for him at home. Norma was pregnant at the time and didn't want to wash a lot of dishes. Herb got very upset and ran away to the bus depot. Norma went and brought him back. I made a movie on my 8mm Kodak camera named "Oy Vey Herbie Came."

Chapter 26
The First Branch Sprouts

On May 3, 1956, a beautiful, clear, blue-sky, spring day with snow still on Pikes Peak and all the trees in full bloom, our first son was born at the Fort Carson hospital (weighing 7 pounds), where Norma had gone for all her prenatal care. The only costs incurred were for Norma's meals at the base hospital, about $7.

We named him Joel Howard in honor of Joel Shapov and my mother, Henny. His birth was a monumental occasion. This was the first step in the resurrection of the Dreifuss family, which, except for me, had been obliterated in Germany.

Sam and Leah came for the bris and stayed for one week. They paid for everything. We set up the bar and food in Lee and Ellen Modjeska's apartment across the hall. Sam made his famous fried chicken and everybody had a great time.

We showed Sam and Leah all the great attractions in Colorado Springs, including Will Rodgers' Shrine. Sam was a big fan of his. They also enjoyed seeing Pikes Peak, Manitou Springs, the Broadmoor Hotel with its zoo, and The Gardens of the Gods where we went often to hear a symphony orchestra play the 1812 overture, using the cannons from Fort Carson.

Five days after Joel was born, Norma's favorite cousin, Hal Mishkin, and his wife, Barbara, who married two years before us, had their first son Gary.

Norma's parents sent us a baby crib, which we kept right next to our bed. When Joel was a few months old, he would pull down the bumper pads and peak at us. The crib lasted for all our children and even our grandchildren when they came to our house for a visit. It was still in fine condition but didn't comply with the new safety codes, so it went.

Front: Paula holding one-month-old Joel, Martin.
Back: Werner, Herbie and Norma.

While we were in Colorado Springs the Hotel Del Coronado underwent remodeling and Paula's Porch Shop closed. Norma's family moved back to Los Angeles. They came for the *Pidyon Ha' Ben*, the official Jewish baby naming, when Joel was one month old.

In October 1956 when Joel was six months old, I received my honorable discharge from the Army, was compensated for 60 days of leave time that I had accumulated, and travel expenses back to San Diego. We packed up the "Grey Ghost," put Joel in a baby bed that fit into the entire back seat and headed to Chula Vista. The first night we stopped in Albuquerque, New Mexico to find a whole case of canned baby milk that we purchased at the post PX was frozen and had to be thrown away.

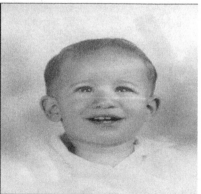

Joel Dreifuss at one year old

Chapter 27-Return to Civilian Life

We arrived to a furnished apartment in National City that Sam was able to find. Housing was in short supply since San Diego was still a Navy town. Six weeks after coming home, Norma had an emergency appendectomy. Joel was very mature for his age and was like a little man by the time he was one year old. His favorite pastime was riding his rocking horse.

Several months later, we found a new unfurnished apartment, Trinity Arms, near 3rd and Highland Avenue in National City, also a short distance from the ranch.

We purchased our first piece of furniture, a two-piece living room set with green tweed fabric and wagon-wheel ends that tilted back to make a bed, and a matching rocker. We also bought a bedroom set and an early American dinette set with two leaves and six yellow flower prints, vinyl-skirted seats for cash at South Coast Plaza at 8th and Highland in National City. Anything we ever purchased, except our homes, was paid for in cash. If we didn't have the cash for an item, we didn't buy it. There were no credit cards at that time.

Fast Forward:

The dinette set lasted for over 25 years and was replaced when we moved into our current home.

Norma, eight-month-old Joel, and Werner

I worked with Sam only for a short time after returning from the army as the size of the ranch and the cattle business were shrinking due to commercial development. In addition, one of Leah's nephews who was a real estate broker, took over the property management while I was in the service.

Chapter 28-Our First New House

While still working with Sam, we bought our first new house for $15,700, which in those days was a lot of money. Monthly payments were $87. It was located on Alvin Street, in a new development called Emerald Hills, close to Euclid and Federal Avenue in San Diego, only a few miles north of the ranch. It was an early American style home, about 900 square feet, with hardwood floors, a living room, three small bedrooms, 1½ baths, a kitchen with all the built-ins, a Bendix washer-dryer combination, and a dinette area overlooking the big backyard.

R. Werner and Joel by the planter box I built
L: Two years later Bob & Joel

Chapter 29
Two More Branches Sprout

Our second son, Robert Michael, was born April 16,1958 at Sharp Hospital in San Diego. Robert was named after Norma's cousin, Robert, whose daughter Carole Ray was our flower girl. Michael was for Norma's uncle, Michael Harris. Dr. Phil Rand delivered him. Bobby, as we call him, was completely opposite from his 2 year-old brother Joel, who had dark hair and was very independent and mature. Bobby was a cuddle bug, had light curly blond hair and liked more attention than Joel. He could find more ways to get into mischief and then smile at Norma and say, "Mommy, you're so beautiful."

Late one night when Bobby was about two years old and everybody was sleeping, Norma woke up feeling a cold draft coming through our bedroom, only to find the refrigerator and back doors wide open and Bobby sound asleep on the back steps. One Memorial Day when he was a year old he flushed his undershorts down the toilet which resulted in a very large plumbing bill.

Our third son, Ted Allan, was due the end of June, but was several weeks late. On July 4th, 1959 Ted was born, delivered by Dr. Rand, at Sharp Hospital and became our firecracker baby.

135

He was completely different from his older brothers. He had a lot of dark hair, was the biggest at birth (nine plus pounds), was very quiet, mild and very sweet with big dimples. We called him our Teddy Bear. He was named after Norma's grandmother, Tema Rosa.

As you can imagine, the house was getting a little crowded, and the neighborhood was undergoing a change. So we bought a new larger house in Point Loma, just north of downtown San Diego, where many of our friends lived.

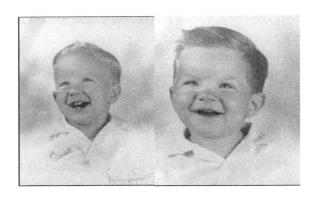

Robert   (one year old) Ted

Chapter 30-Change in Career

In the later part of 1957, I decided that the cattle business in the South Bay and San Diego area was dying and I needed to make a change. The dairies were moving to central California where land was less expensive.

One tenant on the ranch property had a children's midget racecar track, and one of their sponsors was Alvin Strep, owner of Teller's Discount stores. They sold major appliances, furniture, clothing, etc. I made an appointment to see Alvin. He asked me what I could do. I replied, "Anything and everything that needs to be done in your company." I was experienced with personnel from the army, leases, insurance, buying, selling and business in general.

He asked me to return on Wednesday and talk to his partner, Morrie Leibowitz, a CPA from Los Angeles. I wasn't even aware he had a partner.

On Wednesday, I interviewed with Morrie and he hired me on the spot. I think he needed someone reliable to protect his interest. I have no idea how Alvin, of Polish descent, and Morrie from Los Angeles became partners.

I never had any doubts or trepidations about making the change, or for that matter, any future business or financial decisions whatsoever.

The main Teller's store was a two-story building at 11th and University Avenue, across the street from a Sears' store. There was a smaller one-story store at 3rd Avenue and G Street in Chula Vista. They were both much smaller than the current discount stores. Their offices were in a three-story building across the street from their main store and they had a city block sized furniture warehouse in downtown San Diego. All the properties were leased.

Sam never said anything about my decision, but in the back of his mind, he must have known it was the right choice.

My first assignment for Teller's was to subcontract the construction of an addition to the main store, pay all the bills from a special account, and to review all the insurance policies, leases and store security.

Construction was completed in record time and within budget, and Alvin asked me to become the manager of the furniture department, which was the biggest profit maker and occupied the entire second floor of the San Diego store as well as a portion of the Chula Vista store.

One of the biggest selling items was Serta mattress sets, and the store would earn prizes from the Serta Company, which in 1960 included four round trips to Hawaii for five days. Alvin gave two trips to Norma and me and the other two to Bahjat (Jat) Deiranieh and his wife, Ginny. Jat was the manager and buyer for the clothing department and had been with the company for a number of years.

Jat was born in Jordan on March 12, 1930, the same day as I was but one year earlier. Ginny was from Fresno and of Armenian descent. They had two children, Janan who we see quite often, and David.

We became good friends in Hawaii and had a great time. The Reef Hotel was on the beach, which our rooms overlooked, and Serta had many special events for all their guests.

Chapter 31-Selling Our First House

In 1960, I became the manager of Teller's store in Chula Vista. One afternoon, a very clean-cut, young, African-American man came in to buy a set of bunk beds on credit for his children. After filling out the application, I called Seaboard Finance and got approval over the phone. The gentleman was Herb Nash, living in an apartment and working at Rohr Aircraft, the largest employer in Chula Vista. On weekends he was a preacher and did gardening for one of my classmates who I graduated with from Chula Vista High School. I sat him down and told him he needed to buy a home for his family, and I just happened to have just the right one for him. He said he couldn't afford it. I told him to bring his wife over to see it and I would make it affordable.

That evening he came with his wife and three children. They fell in love with the house, its hardwood floors, Bendix washer/dryer combination, great big backyard and the neighborhood. To them, it was a palace. I told them the price and that they could take over the payments on the first mortgage, which was $87 per month and I would finance the second mortgage. The deal was made. He never missed a payment. Herb would come by our store on many occasions to make

the house payment and always thanked me for selling
him the house.

Fast Forward:

*Several years ago, we were in that area and stopped
to see Herb. He was delighted to see us and took us
through the house. They had added a family room in
the back. He had retired from Rohr Aircraft as a driver
of an 18-wheeler from the Chula Vista to the Riverside
location. His wife had passed away, he remarried, and
all the children had grown and moved out. He was still
a preacher.*

When Teller's closed the Chula Vista store, I
transferred back to the main store to manage the
furniture department on a deal that included wages plus
a percentage of the profits. Teller's had opened an
Annex across the street from the main store at 11th, and
University that sold mainly clothing and small
appliances that Jat managed.

Teller's had been trying to emulate discount stores
in Los Angeles but was spending too much for
advertising, especially appliances, and not making
enough profit. In late 1960, Teller's closed, as did the
stores in Los Angeles.

The furniture department was profitable until the
closing day, and I was able to get all the money owed to
me from the profit percentage in the way of furniture
for our Point Loma house.

Chapter 32-The Bargain Center

Jat and I made a deal with Alvin Strep to buy Teller's Annex, which contained a large inventory of clothing, small electrical appliances, miscellaneous merchandise, fixtures, large stainless steel rectangular baskets which we hung on pegboard and put on the tables, National cash registers, marking machines, etc. for $10,000. Jat paid half and I borrowed $5000 from Lilian Hamill who, with her late husband, Tom, had owned a cleaning business at the ranch. Our plan was to be merchandise liquidators. The demise of Teller's gave birth to my new business, The Bargain Center.

Opportunity came knocking and we opened the door.

There was a month-to-month lease on the annex property, and the owner had plans to tear down the building. My friend, Zane Feldman, Alice's husband, informed me of a vacant Piggly Wiggly grocery store on Wightman Street, just across from his San Diego Fabrics store at the corner of 30th & Wightman Street in North Park, one block south of University Avenue. It had been vacant for more than six months, since the Piggly Wiggly grocery store chain owned by DD Williams was bought by Buy and Save, which closed many small stores, including this location. Jat and I checked it out and contacted the trust department handling the property for the DD Williams estate, which had retained the property. We negotiated and leased the 4500 sq. ft. building including the 4500 sq. ft. parking lot at the corner of Wightman and Ray Street for $400 per month. It was one block south and one block east of 30th and University Avenue, the main corner of the North Park business district. They painted the building inside and out, resurfaced and fenced the parking lot and put in new front doors.

We had signs painted on the inside walls saying, "Here Prices Are Born Not Raised" and "Anything You Want We Might Have, If Not Today Maybe Tomorrow." The sign painter was a funny, small, African American man with a goatee, named Mitch. He also painted our outside signs and did a great job.

The brick building had a 50-foot front with a canopy covering part of the six-foot sidewalk, was 90-feet deep and had a high ceiling with glass block windows on both sides, and a skylight in the middle. This construction saved on lighting bills and was standard for all Piggly Wiggly stores in the San Diego area, most of which are still standing. This one was built in March 1939.

North Park had been a major shopping district with many fine quality men's and ladies' clothing stores, several shoe stores, sporting goods and jewelry shops, most of which were owned by Jewish people, as well as major chains such as The Limited, Woolworths, J C Penney, Leeds, See's Candy, National Dollar, Thrifty Drugstore, Mayfair and other markets, and several major banks.

The residents were mainly middle-aged living in small homes built in the early 1920s. When the large Mission Valley shopping center opened just several miles north, it had a major detrimental financial effect on the area.

We hired one of Teller's general repairman to put peg-board on the walls with shelves on top and do some electrical work.

We moved the entire Teller's Annex including all the merchandise and fixtures to the North Park location in two days and were fortunate to be able to hire some of the employees from Teller's who had worked in Jat's department as well as their accountant, Allen Wexler. One of the employees was Marg Harvey, who was part Native American and a very strong, smart woman. Her son, Doug Harvey, was a well-known major league baseball umpire.

The buzz on the Main Street, University Avenue, was that these two young whippersnappers on the back street would be gone in six months. This was in early 1961. The store is still there, while most of the individual owned and chain stores are long gone. Many of those stores didn't have heirs to take over the business and the rents became too expensive.

Diego Independent, Thursday, April 27, 1961   Page 21 (M-E)

Werner and Jat

The only other continuing family-owned store is A & B Sporting Goods, on the corner of University and Ray Street, one block from our store. Dave and Ann Schloss started the business in 1941 and Joe, their son, took it over when Dave passed away and operated it with his son Greg.

Joe coached the North Park little league team for over 60 years and the city mayor proclaimed May 16, 2015 as Joe Schloss day. He was honored and presented with many awards for his years of voluntary services.

Joe passed away November 25, 2015 at the age of 88. The city named a street "Joe Schloss Way," near Morley Field, in his honor after his death.

.

Grand opening April 1961

Our son, Joel, is also an avid baseball player as was Joel Shapov. When he was about 10 years old, he loved to come with me to our store. He helped with working the cash register, and enjoyed going to the sporting goods store. Dave would always tell him to ask me for a raise.

The Bargain Center became a general merchandise liquidation store. Back in the 1960s, traveling sales representatives were still the lifeblood of most wholesale companies. Jat had many connections in the clothing industry, having been the buyer at Teller's, and we would buy closeouts, salesman samples from many jobbers, slight irregulars in towels, clothing, boots, etc. We would also buy at auction, entire stores that San Diego Men's Wholesale Credit Association had taken over, one of which was a Robert Hall men's store with a large inventory of good quality men's clothing and fixtures that we moved into our store.

Another great resource was West Coast Liquidators in Los Angeles, which sold boxed greeting and Christmas cards, plastic Christmas trees, house-wear items, and a great variety of other things. They later became retailers, Pick & Save and then Big Lots.

The store always had the entire back page of a tabloid for the North Park merchant district in the weekly Independent newspaper, owned by Elliot Cushman. He is a grandson of Adolf Levi. The paper closed many years ago, and Elliot went into the auto dealership business which sold a few years ago and is now a partner in Cushman & Wakefield Real Estate.

We also advertised in the Union-Tribune. Since there were only a few discount stores, people would drive a long way for bargains. We were paying rent seven days a week, we were open seven days a week. Jat and I alternated working on Sundays.

Dun & Bradstreet, of course, wanted a financial statement, which we provided. It wasn't the most favorable since we had been in business only for a very short period of time.

To this day, they never received another financial statement. When we encountered a new vendor, I simply gave them the names of our current vendors and suppliers, and the merchandise was shipped. The store's bills were always paid on time and before we withdrew any money for ourselves.

In February 1963, Jat wanted to sell his share of the business and go into business with one of his fellow citizens from Jordan. We always got along very well and never had a cross word. We took inventory and settled at the price of $18,000, which I borrowed from the Security Bank, with Sam Shapov's guarantee on the loan.

Here I was, the owner of my own business at the age 31, just 21 years after coming to America without a penny in my pocket. **What a wonderful country, you come without a penny and within a few years, you can owe a fortune.**

Sam Shapov died on March 8, 1963 at the age of 66, one month after I bought out my partner. The bank notified me that Leah withdrew the guarantee, I'm sure her nephew instigated that. This actually had no effect unless I had tried to renew it, which never happened. Either way I could have renewed the loan without her guarantee. I paid the loan as per the agreement and never asked her ever again for any favors.

Prior to the new 805-freeway opening, Wightman Street was renamed as North Park Way and brand new entrance and exit sign were put up. Bargain Center's address became 3015 North Park Way. To our benefit the "back street" no longer existed and our traffic increased considerably.

Back in the early 1960s, most of the clothing wholesalers, jobbers and manufactures were located on South Los Angeles Street and surrounding areas. I had some excellent suppliers for men's suits and sports coats, a gigantic business for us for many years. Many local politicians, including Congressional representatives, doctors and other professional people were our customers. When the traditional leisure suits became the rage, we phased out the suit business. I had contact with many great sources, most of which are long gone, one being "Prince of Hollywood," owned by Art Emory. Many jobbers disliked him, but to me he was an angel. He had an "in" with Farah Manufacturing and bought all their closeouts, overruns, and slightly irregular slacks, jeans and shorts at fantastically low prices. I bought them in big lots at less than half of the wholesale price and was able to retail them at the original wholesale price. Art also had an "in" with "Dotty Dan" in La Mesa, Texas, which manufactured an extremely fine line of infant and toddler clothing. I bought large boxes of their closeouts, overruns, and slight irregulars at $6 per dozen. It was like Christmas opening some of the boxes which included toddler wool coats, velvet holiday dresses, toddler outfits, etc.

I would ask Art, "When would you like me to pay you?" and his reply was always the same, "Pay when you can." He knew he would always be paid in 30 days or less. There was never a limit as to as to how much I could buy.

I would drive up to Los Angeles early in the morning in our 9-passenger Dodge Monaco station wagon, the first new car I ever bought, and do my buying, load up as much as I could, have the balance shipped, and be back at the store by 3 o'clock p.m.

Twice a year Norma and I would attend a trade show in Las Vegas, The Associate Surplus Dealers (ASD), on their $39 package deal for a three-day, two-night stay at the Dune's Hotel, a luncheon for the women, and a cocktail dinner party for all. Besides the wholesale Military Surplus dealers, there were many manufacturers and importers selling closeout goods, and the numbers kept growing.

As it got bigger, (over 6000 booths), the show moved to the Las Vegas Hilton and Sands Convention Center. Of course, the price for the package deal kept going up over the years too.

I continued buying entire businesses of all kinds.

Chapter 33
The Shapov Family Trust

It was on a Friday evening, March 8, 1963, when all stores in North Park stayed open until 9 pm and I received a call that Sam Shapov had died at a convalescent hospital in Lemon Grove. He was 66 and had been recovering from an encounter with a bull that had thrown him over a fence. Sam's niece, Elena, had visited him several days before his passing. She told me Sam informed her about his and Leah's trust and instructed her to make sure Leah didn't change it if he should die.

Shortly after Sam's death, his widowed sister-in-law, Ida, Elena's mother, and her five children filed suit against Leah to prevent her from changing the trust, and they prevailed. In June 1964, Leah signed the agreement. Leah continued to live in the house on C Street with live-in help in later years. She was active, mainly financially, at Temple Beth Shalom on Madrona Street in Chula Vista where Sam was one of the founding members and past president. I called her every morning and picked her up for all of our family festivities and celebrations such as birthdays, holidays, etc.

Leah loved sweets, especially candy and ice cream,

even though she was a diabetic. I visited her on December 26, 1977 in a hospital while she was undergoing dialysis; I kissed her and told her that I loved her. She died that day. Ironically, Norma's mother, Paula, passed away on December 26th in 1990 at 88 years old. Her cousin Lil also died on December 26.

The Shapov charitable trust was set up with 100 shares assigned to 33 individual beneficiaries as well as four charities that will split the balance upon the death of the last beneficiary. Five percent of the value of the estate, at the time of Leah's death, is to be distributed semiannually to the 33 beneficiaries and charities. It amounts to less than $63,000 total. It never changes but its value reduces with inflation and everyone is required to pay taxes on that income. I never knew about the trust nor did I feel it was my right to inquire about it, as I was a guest in the Shapov home for six years. This did not give me the right to dictate how their assets were to be distributed or if I was even entitled.

Did I fill the void in their home and hearts created by Joel's death? I hope so.

Did I accord them the respect, as their own child would have? I think so.

Did I always look out for their best interests? Yes.

Did they appreciate that we named our first-born Joel? How could they not? Did I give them reasons to be proud of my accomplishments, wife and children so that Leah always signed greeting cards "from Grandma Leah"? Without question. How could they not?

The distribution of the trust tells its own story and is as follows:

Leah's nephew, Babe, received 15 shares and his two daughters, three shares each. All three of them have passed away. Babe's only granddaughter received two shares, all for a total of 23 shares.

I received 13 shares and our four children, combined, nine shares for a total of 22 shares, which is gratifying. It's like found money.

Sam's widowed sister-in-law, Ida, and four of her grown children and one grandniece received a total of 18 shares. The remaining nephews, nieces and a few other individuals each received one or two shares.

Sam had a sister and a brother living in Latvia who are acknowledged in the will, however, without any provisions for them. They filed a suit that was dismissed.

Northern Trust has administered the trust extremely well and its value has grown substantially, always paying the beneficiaries on time.

<u>Chapter 34-Diversification</u>

In August 1965, when the Watts riots took place in Los Angeles, I decided it was time to diversify and not have all my assets in my business. I contacted a friend who was a stockbroker and I asked about the airlines. He advised that I buy Pan Am, PSA, and American and I bought 10 shares of each. I think he made more commission by selling three stocks instead of one. I made a profit on PSA and American that covered the loss I encountered when Pan Am that went bankrupt.

Norma's cousin, Hy, from Los Angeles would always talk about his stocks whenever we saw him. He would give me tips on Canadian penny stocks that would turn out to be worthless. I bought many stocks over the years, some that turned out to be dogs, but many more that were very profitable.

One of the first rules I followed was never buy stocks with money I would ever need, as well as to learn from my mistakes, which I did. When the market goes down, which it does, you can just sit back and wait for the recovery and buy more at a lower price. In the long run, the market will go up to keep pace with inflation. The stock market is similar to a baseball game. One doesn't score in every inning but winning the game is what counts.

Over the years I have owned shares of many companies, some of which I have held for years and encountered many stock splits such as Adobe Systems and Philip Morris that resulted in owning five quality companies that pay close to 5% dividends.

Highly appreciated stocks are an excellent way to make charitable donations. It's a win-win situation. Gifting stocks to members of the family is also a great way to distribute wealth. They are less likely to sell the stocks, whereas they most likely would spend a cash gift.

Chapter 35-Point Loma House

Our new open-beamed, one-story home on Larga Circle in the Point Loma area of San Diego was considerably larger than the previous house and cost approximately $22,000. It was on a cul-de-sac, which was great for the children to play. It had a kitchen with a breakfast counter, a large dining room/living room with sliding glass doors on the left side leading to the backyard and three large bedrooms on the right side of the house.

Since we lived close to the ocean, the air was very damp and musty. One day Norma called me at the store to tell me there were mushrooms growing out of the walls in the bathroom. I thought she was hallucinating and told her I'd take care of it. I sprayed the walls with weed killer, but the mushrooms kept on growing.

We built a room in the garage for a housekeeper, one of which we discovered was enjoying our liquor and refilling the bottles with tea. She became history.

We lived in Point Loma for three years. Joel started kindergarten the last year, and our daughter, Marsi, was born.

Chapter 36-Birth of Marsi

Our daughter, Marsi Jan, was born on May 6, 1962 at Sharp Hospital on Kearney Mesa where Bobby and Ted were born. Dr. Phil Rand also delivered her.

Having a girl, after three boys, was quite an exciting event. Many of our close friends and relatives had only boys, including Norma's favorite cousin Hal Mishkin whose wife, Barbara, gave birth to their third son, Greg, the same day as Marsi was born. We call them twin cousins.

Marsi was named after Norma's farther, Martin Simmons, who passed away on October 31, 1959. The day Norma came home from the hospital, as a surprise that evening, Edie, and her husband Dean Greenberg, along with Alice and Zane Feldman and many of our close friends and family came marching into our house to celebrate. They came with baby presents, food, paper plates and a big cake with pink booties made from cream cheese designed and created by Edie Greenberg. Norma still has the booties in our freezer.

Norma had a ball dressing Marsi with all the gifts and mostly in the beautiful clothes from "Dotty Dan Manufacturer" that I sold in our store. You might say Marsi was a little bit spoiled. She really was a tomboy having no sisters and three older brothers. Marsi was the only one of our children ever to break an arm. She is still spoiled.

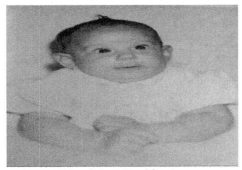

Marsi Jan Dreifuss

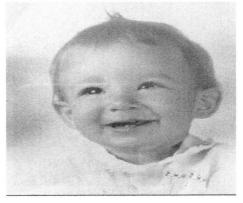

Marsi at one year old

Hal and Barbara Mishkin's 80th birthday & 60th
Wedding anniversary party in Santa Barbara
February 2013

Marsi (Dreifuss) Frenkel and Greg Mishkin (twin
cousins) February 2013

Chapter 37-College Gardens House

In 1964, we decided to move inland because of the damp cold days and the Point Loma house was in the direct flight path from Lindberg Field.

While looking for a new house, our friend Zane Feldman told us that College Gardens Court, just four blocks from their house in the San Diego State College area, had been extended and 15 new homes were being built.

We bought one of the larger tri-level models for $36,500 with the builder carrying back the second mortgage, which we paid off several years later at a big discount. Many of our other friends also lived in this area. It was in an excellent school district and the air was not damp like it was in Point Loma.

The main level of the house included a living/dining room, kitchen with an eating counter, dinette area and a half bath for guests. Downstairs we had a large family room with a pool table, a wet bar and sliding glass doors to the back patio, Joel's bedroom, a full bathroom and the garage, where again, we built a new room for a housekeeper. The upstairs had a large master bedroom overlooking our backyard and the canyon, the master bathroom, two bedrooms, one for Marsi, and the other shared by Bobby and Ted and a full bathroom. Both bedrooms were above the garage and facing the street. We planted fruit trees and had a garden on the upper level of the backyard. The lower level was our patio.

We sold our Point Loma house for about the same price as we had paid for it, then had to reprocess it, and sold it again at a higher price.

Hardy Elementary School was within walking distance from our home. For one year, all four of our children were enrolled there, Marsi in kindergarten, Joel in 6th grade and Bob and Ted in-between.

The kids kept asking for a dog, so one day I found one advertised in the Penny Saver and brought him home. He was an older bulldog about 8-inches wide and looked like an end table. The kids were all sitting at the dinner table when I brought him in and all started running in different directions when they saw him. I took him back. He was not what they wanted.

I found another dog, a mixed-breed terrier puppy that the owner had named Monster since he was always climbing out of his box. He had trained him to put out cigarette butts. We never needed him to do so since no one in our family smoked nor do they today, with the exception of our free spirit son Bobby who likes to smoke joints.

The kids really liked Monster. He was a great watchdog. The first night after getting him, we had a discussion at the dinner table to decide on his name. Each of the kids wanted a different name and started to cry when their suggestion wasn't chosen.

I finally said that "Monster" will continue to be his name and everybody was happy. There was only one problem. We use to refer to Bobby as "Monster" because he was always getting into mischief.

Monster slept with Joel until he left for college, He slept with Bobby until we moved him to the room in the garage with his waterbed and all his belongings. Bobby painted the room blue, played his loud music and it was much more peaceful in the house. I asked Norma never to go into his room and only do his washing when he brought it out.

Monster then slept with Ted until he moved to a fraternity house at San Diego State College and finally with Marsi, who would never before allow him on her bed. Sometimes when the kids were young, they would all climb into our bed, including Monster. We had him for 14 years.

Once when we came home from a vacation, Norma's mother, Paula, had stayed with the kids, the housekeeper and Michael, Norma's nephew. The first thing they told us when we got home was that Grandma Paula had given Monster an aspirin because she thought he had a headache. Monster wouldn't let Paula get near the kids without growling. He was very protective of the kids.

When Joel was 11, he started a Union-Tribune morning paper route, as did Bobby. During summer break from high school, Joel would often work at our

store and he also took a job at Bagel World, owned by friends of ours. Bobby worked part time at a friend's father's air-conditioning business. After Bobby graduated from school, he started his own air-conditioning business, which he knows very well. Ted worked at Baskin-Robbins and at a bicycle shop.
The boys were very good at handling their money. At 16, Joel bought his first new car for $2700. a brown two-door Capri manufactured by Ford. After high school graduation, Joel went to college in Santa Cruz where we helped him buy a condominium.

Bobby bought a used Mazda pick-up when he was 16 for $2400 and rebuilt the engine in our garage. He bought an old house and remodeled it at 18 years old without any help from us. Then he built two units in the rear. Several years later the state needed the property to build a freeway and Bobby bought another house that he also remodeled and added a units.

Ted bought a used VW bug for $700. With Bobby's help, they made it into a Baja Bug in our garage and had it painted bright orange.

I was amazed that they got it all back together.

Joel, Bob, Marsi, Ted & Monster   Werner and Norma
at the store 1964

Chapter 38
Tifereth Israel Synagogue

While we were living on College Gardens Court in the San Diego State University area, we became members at Tifereth Israel Synagogue on 30th and Howard Street in North Park. Tifereth synagogue is where Norma and I were married, and where, in 1944, I became a Bar Mitzvah.

All of our children attended Sunday and Hebrew school and were Bar and Bat Mitzvah'd with Rabbi Levens, officiating.

The boys had big dinner/dance parties, Joel's and Ted's at the El Cortez Hotel, where Adolph Levi had lived and where I took Norma on our first date. Bobby had his at the Royal Inn at the wharf. Marsi had a lunch party at Sea World restaurant. So all family members could attend, Norma and I also made a Bar Mitzvah in San Diego at our synagogue, and a dinner party at the Town and Country for Michael, our nephew, who was living in Denver with his mother.

Paying for four children to attend Sunday and Hebrew school, sisterhood and membership dues, came to quite an expense. There wasn't much left over to make a donation to Tifereth. In lieu of doing so, I gave my time and talent. I served on the board of directors for 20 years, and served as vice president in 1979 during the transition of selling the location in North Park and building a new synagogue on Tommy Drive and Cowls Mountain in La Mesa. Chuck Schwartz was president at that time and we ran the bingo games, which raised a considerable amount of money. Several years before, I served as chairman of the New Building Fund auction, which brought in close to $10,000.

This undertaking was somewhat of life-changing experience. I had always been rather mild tempered but while trying to obtain auction items like a 3-day stay at a hotel people wished us well but mostly replied with a "no thanks." I became very assertive and angry, and didn't let up until they gave us an auction item.

Letter of regret to my 50th birthday party from Chuck, president of the congregation, about says it all.

February 21, 1981

Dear Werner,

HAPPY 49TH PLUS

Sorry we could not be with you, but duty calls. I know that you understand the meaning of that. How many times you answered the same call is beyond counting. Your enthusiasm and dedication to your family, your business, and your synagogue are of the highest magnitude. Carnival, Auction, moving of the Shul, the dedication, the Ground breaking, Men's club, Fund Raisings, meetings, meetings and more meetings. It goes on and on.

Your energy is boundless and usually outlasts the rest of us. Whatever you eat for breakfast should be shared with all of us. I am sure Norma can attest to it better than we can, but then again no family secrets. We would much rather be with you tonight celebrating your 50th birthday, but since we cannot, we surely want you to know that we wish you:

* Long Life * Happiness*and sales of 1000 mopeds this year.

All our love,

Chuck and Barbara Sue Schwartz

Werner at the new synagogue brick building November 1978

Chapter 39
Norma Follows Her Dream in Fashion

In 1975, Joel was away at college, Bobby had moved to his own house, Ted and Marsi were in high school and Bullock's Department store was opening a new store in Mission Valley, San Diego.

Norma had majored in business administration and women's dress design at UCLA, and had worked for May Co. in Los Angeles as a teenager. She told me she would like to go to work part-time in the ladies fashion department at the new Bullock's store. She applied before the store was opened and they hired her immediately. Before the stores grand opening the management asked her to work full time. Norma and I discussed it, we talked to the store manager and we agreed she'd work full time providing they would give her time off whenever we wanted to travel, to which they agreed.

Norma loved working there and was the top sales associate every year. She won many prizes including a trip for two to Hawaii, which was exchanged for a trip to Hong Kong, a Magnavox stereo, silver platters, money, additional discounts and many plaques for her outstanding customer service.

Norma

We had a great relationship with the Bullocks store managers, and they never gave us any problems as to Norma taking time off. She stayed on as an hourly salary employee rather than a fixed salary manager since the store had a habit of working their employees many more hours than their scheduled time.

There was only one problem; it was costing me a fortune to have her working there with all the additional taxes to be paid and all the merchandise she was buying. She retired as a department manager in 1992.

Chapter 40
The Mopeds and Store Building

In 1987, a nice young man came into the store and introduced himself as a beneficiary of the DD Williams Trust and owned the building. He told me he lived on a boat off Sausalito, California. He bought some items and I gave him a discount. The following year he returned, informed me the trust had been dissolved and he had obtained the Bargain Center property. I told him if he ever wanted to sell it, to let me know.

As I mentioned before, twice a year we attended a three-day trade show in Las Vegas. In 1979, several weeks before the summer show, our son, Ted, who was attending San Diego State College, decided to buy a moped. After checking all the dealers, he bought a used one from a private party. Half-joking, he said to me, "You ought to buy some mopeds for the store." I didn't even know what a moped was and never gave it a second thought.

When Norma and I walked into the Vegas trade show, which had about 6000 booths selling everything under the sun, we first saw our friend, Norm Fisch from San Diego. He was standing by a display of several Garelli mopeds. Norm had just started working as a sales representative for Barter International in Los Angeles, which had acquired the entire inventory of several thousand units from the authorized US Garelli distributor, who wanted out of the business. The mopeds were not selling well. They were warehoused in five different locations: Los Angeles, Minneapolis, New Jersey and several others. One of the stipulations was that Barter International was prohibited from selling the mopeds to the authorized retail Garelli dealers. Therefore, they had to find other sources to sell even thou the dealers had to honor the factory warranty.

After getting some information from Norm, I proceeded to go about doing my regular buying from my usual sources as well as scouting for new items. At that time, the store was still a general merchandise liquidation operation.

Whenever I had time, I would return to Norm's booth and get more information about the mopeds. They were priced about $100 dollars below the regular wholesale, selling in lots of 25 or more, at an even larger discount.

There were three models: the 2-passenger VIP step-through that came in bright yellow, metallic blue, bright red, and white, the one-passenger step-through in the same colors; and a one-passenger motorcycle style that came in black or dark green. All had oil injectors for mixing two-stroke oil with the gas for the 50cc engine and didn't require a special driver's license.

They were boxed in sturdy 10-inch wide, five-foot-long and three-foot-high boxes, completely assembled except for the front wheel, handle bar, and foot pedals.

I told Norm I wanted to check out the local dealer and would get back to him after we returned home. I went to the San Diego dealer who was located only 4 miles from our store. The Garelli seemed like an excellent moped. I called Norm and ordered 25 but asked him to ship 12 immediately and the balance at a later date, to which he agreed. It was a big job making room even for the first lot.

My employees set up one of each style and color, and displayed them in front of the store. They started selling and I then had the other 13 shipped. Not only did we sell the mopeds, but I had to find sources for accessories such as turn signals, windshields, three kinds of baskets, cable locks, mirrors, foot pegs, two-stroke oil, gas cans, bumper mounts, helmets, gloves, goggles and service manuals. These accessories could add $100 or more to the sale.

Later on, we sold tires, tubes, cables, and bulbs and we also did minor service when needed.

We were selling them for about $100 less than the dealer. I got rather excited and told Norm I wanted to try to buy the entire inventory of approximately 500 sitting in the Los Angeles warehouse. I suggested that we drive up there on Sunday. Norm said, "They won't do it", but I insisted and we drove up to L.A.

I offered to pay a $15,000 deposit on the entire lot in Los Angeles, pay for the mopeds as I withdrew them and leave a deposit for the last batch. The deposit would be theirs if I didn't take them all by a certain date. They accepted my offer, drew up the contract and I signed it. Within several weeks, I had my new business completely under control.

A few weeks later, the gas shortage came and was causing long lines at the gas stations, higher prices and all hell broke loose at the store. We couldn't set up mopeds fast enough and sold many in boxes at a slightly lower price. We had the warehouse ship 50 mopeds every few days.

We opened Sundays and stayed late the other days. Bobby, Ted, Marsi and even Norma came to the store to help. Joel was still away at school. It was so busy during the day, I wrote ads at night for the Union-Tribune and the Independent papers with borders saying "Put Your Money in the Bank, Not in the Tank."

When the original lot of mopeds I had purchased was depleting, I ordered an additional truckload, 173 mopeds, from the Minneapolis warehouse. They were shipped cross-country piggyback on a flatbed rail car, then in San Diego they hitched to a tractor and drove to the store. It took the driver and two of my employees half a day just to unload them, make room and stack in the back of the store. The freight cost was only about $10 each.

I had gone to my banker around the corner from the store and asked for a short-term loan of $75,000 to buy the load.

He said I needed to fill out a financial statement, which I had never done in almost 20 years of banking with them. I told him why bother since I was a long-time customer and if I couldn't get the loan on my reputation, I was banking at the wrong bank. He looked at me and said, "The money will be in your account this afternoon." I paid it back in 30 days. That was the only time I ever borrowed money for the business.

During this time, we started buying back Garelli mopeds from our customers as well as purchasing other used brands. Many people bought them not only for driving around town, but also to put on their campers. I bought two VIP models exactly five years from the date we sold them, one with five miles and the other with seven miles.

The San Diego chicken, mascot for the Padre's, was a costumer of ours and used one of our mopeds to drag the infield during half time at the games.

I rode my VIP moped to the store almost every day. It was great fun.

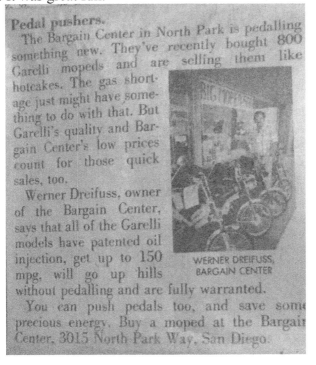

Pedal pushers.

The Bargain Center in North Park is pedalling something new. They've recently bought 800 Garelli mopeds and are selling them like hotcakes. The gas shortage just might have something to do with that. But Garelli's quality and Bargain Center's low prices count for those quick sales, too.

Werner Dreifuss, owner of the Bargain Center, says that all of the Garelli models have patented oil injection, get up to 150 mpg, will go up hills without pedalling and are fully warranted.

WERNER DREIFUSS, BARGAIN CENTER

You can push pedals too, and save some precious energy. Buy a moped at the Bargain Center, 3015 North Park Way, San Diego.

Featured in Retail Trends of the San Diego Union
on July 27, 1979

During this busy time the owner of the Bargain Center building called, saying that he wanted to sell it. "How much do you want?" I asked. He gave me the amount to which I replied, "I'll take it." "How do you want to handle the financing?" I asked. He said, "I'll talk to my accountant and get back to you."

Several days later, he called and informed me of the terms, to which I agreed. He mailed me the papers and the deal was completed. I paid him off in 42 months.

Again, opportunity knocked and I opened the door.

Chapter 41-The Dental Building

Several years later, one of the employees from Dr. Campbell's dental office next to my store advised me they were closing their office. They had done the same with their downtown San Diego location. I asked for the phone number to their main office in Los Angeles.

This one-story corner building of 5000 square feet was built in 1931, had a 50-ft. frontage with the main entrance on 30th Street and 100 ft. frontage on North Park Way, with 2 employee entrances. There is a 4-foot walk-through between the dental building and our stores building.

Dr. Campbell had a chain of dental offices throughout California that only made dentures and gave free credit with a lifetime guarantee. His patients would come from hundreds of miles away.

When he died, his sons decided to close all the offices and liquidate the properties. I called the business manager and advised him that I owned the property next door, and would be interested in acquiring the building. He said he would get back to me, which he never did.

The next thing I knew, in September there was a sale sign on the building. I called the agent to inquire as to the price. It was close to the price I had in mind, but decided to make a lower offer, which they declined.

On December 15, the real estate agent came into our store and told me that they wanted an offer and needed to close escrow by December 31.The agent had no idea if there was any financing on the property however after some research I discovered there were several mortgages held by attorneys. Time was of the essence so I made a lower offer that I knew they would accept, and they did. I assumed the existing mortgages

As soon as I closed escrow, I contacted the attorneys holding and advised them that unless they lowered the 14% interest, I would pay it off in full. The interest was reduced.

Two weeks after I bought the property, I leased it to a dentist and several dentists have occupied it since then.

Again, opportunity knocked and I opened the door.

Chapter 42-Del Cerro House

Ted, our youngest son, was living in a fraternity house at San Diego State College. Our daughter Marsi was attending college at California State University in Northridge and our house on College Gardens Court was rather large for only Norma and me. In addition, the traffic from San Diego State College was steadily increasing and our 14 year-old dog, Monster, had passed away.

We had been looking at new homes built in Del Cerro Heights. It's a gated community that was built in four stages. The first two condominium units were two attached, the third units were single tri-level homes, mostly on the side of a hill. Our friends, Alice and Zane Feldman, had bought one of these several years earlier.

The fourth unit was built a few years later when Jimmy Carter was president and interest rates were about 18%. There were 24 red-tiled-roofs, individual homes, half of which were two stories and several on a two-lot parcel. The other condos across the street were two stories, on the side of a hill and had no back yards.

Norma and I had gone through the model many times but the builder didn't want to take our house in trade. They were asking around $300,000 and had only sold four of the units. This was in 1983. The complex was only one mile from the 8 Freeway and seven miles to our store.

One evening Zane Feldman called to tell us that the builder had returned the 20 remaining units back to the bank, who in turn assigned them to Mission Valley Real Estate to sell. They were going on the market the following day. All the units had to be sold at the same reduced price of $183,000 each, regardless of their condition, for the deal to go through. Ten tri-level units had slopes for backyards and the other 10 had backyards, and were also two-stories.

Zane's neighbor, Lew, had been the sale rep for the builder and was the one we had been talking to for almost a year. He was put in charge of all sales. The models were completely finished with all the built-in appliances, flooring, lighting fixtures and front landscaping, which the others did not have. Of the two remaining, we wanted one of them.

Zane got Lew out of bed, and Norma and I met him at the model house we liked that was on two lots. We walked around it and I gave him a check of $20,000 as deposit, which was required.

We liked this house not only because it was on two lots, completely finished, ready to move into, but also because it had a street light in front, no speed bumps to drive over and had a fantastic view from the balcony in front of the living room and the entire front of the main floor.

Norma thought that was the last of the $20,000 we would ever see.

We called Ernie Addleson and told him to buy one. All the units similar to ours were sold out early the next morning. Ernie put a deposit on one of the sold units, the first buyer didn't qualify, and he got it.

Within several days, all the cliff units sold and the deal with the bank went though.

Again, opportunity knocked and I opened the door.

Fast Forward:

Alice and Zane moved in to a one-story home about a mile away and we, Lew, Ernie and Ellen still live there.

Chapter 43-The Family Tree Grows

Joel was in Santa Cruz working at a deli when he met a young woman. They got married on October 25, 1981. It was a very nice wedding.

On February 26, 1983, their first daughter, our first grandchild, Amy Rebecca Dreifuss, was born. When Amy was one month old, Norma and I met them in Santa Barbara at Norma's cousins, Hal and Barbara's Pacific Crest motel.

When Amy was six months old, I'm sure with Norma's prompting, Joel and his family moved to San Diego into our house on College Gardens Court. Joel began working with me in our store.

We had already moved into our new home in Del Cerro. I would ride my moped to Joel's house, pick him up on his moped and ride together to the store.

They lived there for about one year and then decided to buy a house in Scripps Ranch, north of San Diego. It was a new neighborhood for younger families.

We sold the house on College Gardens Court and used the proceeds to pay off our own new house.

On November 17, 1984, our first grandson, Daniel Aaron, was born. He is the only one of Joel's children who resembles me, and he represents the third generation of the new Dreifuss family.

On April 11, 1988, Jeffrey and Janine were born. Jeff was the bigger of the two and talked for Janine as they got older. They had their own private language only the two of them understood. Norma gave Janine her first bath at the hospital.

Fast Forward:

In February 1994, I told Joel that Norma and I were going on a cruise from Fort Lauderdale through the Panama Canal and ending in San Diego. It was on the Crown Princess, departing on April 30. He suggested we take Amy and Daniel along. I said gladly, if you could get them out of school. Their school consented as long as each of them kept a daily journal of their activities and ports. We flew to Fort Lauderdale several days early and saw the Seminole Indians Village, whom Daniel happened to be studying, and took a boat ride in the Everglades.

April 30, 1994 cruise. Norma & Werner boarding the Crown Princess with Daniel (Mr. Peepers) and Amy

Kids & me on banana boat, and formal night

The kids were an absolute pleasure to have with us. Our cabin had two sets of bunk beds and they slept on the tops of each. There were only two other much younger children aboard with 1500 adults. Amy was like a mother hen, just like at home, and would pick out Daniel's clothes every day, comb his hair and make sure he wrote in his journal daily. After breakfast, Daniel would go up to the top deck and play basketball with the young adults.

The first stop was Princess Cays, Bahamas where we tendered in, enjoyed the beach, swimming and a barbeque lunch. Amy and Daniel went exploring and returned shortly all exited to tell us there were banana floats and suggested to go for a ride. I said no way.

"Aw grandpa, we have to go". And we did. It was a double unit pulled by a motorboat around the roped-off area of the beautiful beach, and it was fun.

At dinner every night, the kids had steak and French fries, ate in a hurry and went to the show room to get front seats, hoping to be picked for the show if the entertainer needed someone from the audience.

One evening at dinner, Daniel asked if I could loan him $95 to buy a new skateboard when we got home. I asked him what kind of collateral he had. "What's collateral, grandpa?" So I gave him his first lesson about finances. Nothing more was said about it.

A few stops later in Aruba, we went to a hotel's beach, the kids, again, found banana floats. "Grandpa, we need to go again!" These were very large single tubes with handles on top. Of course, here we go again. Everyone had a life jacket and one attendant drove the boat pulling us while the other watched us. They took the three of us out in the rough sea, made a sharp turn, maybe on purpose, and all three of us went into the water. Amy started to cry, and I told her just to paddle her feet while the boat came back around. The attendant got in the water and helped Amy and Daniel back on. It was a job for me to get back on since the side of the boat was so slippery. Of course, grandpa had to buy t-shirts saying, "I survived the banana boat spill."

The kids participated in all the events at the pool. In the talent show, Amy dressed like the Captain, wearing his hat and singing, "What I would do if I was the captain of the ship" which she wrote herself.

They spent a lot of time in the pool which had a bar extending into it. They would order Shirley Temples and fight to sign the bills. When we got our halfway statement and I saw the bill, I told them that I forgot to mention, whoever signed the tab had to pay for it. "Aw grandpa" was their response. They knew I was joking. We never had any problem with them. They were always well behaved.

One day near the end of the cruise after lunch, we didn't see Daniel all afternoon. All of a sudden he comes to the cabin all excited with a handful of money. Several of the young adults he played basketball with asked him to go to the Bingo game and watch their cards while they were having a few drinks. They won three Jackpots for the likes of $750 and gave Daniel $250. At dinner that night, I told him now he had money for the new skateboard. At the end of the cruise in San Diego, he couldn't get off the ship fast enough to tell his mother about his winnings.

Amy graduated high school in 2001 and went on to Purdue University in Indiana where she graduated in 4 years. She earned a Bachelor's of Science in Sales, Selling and Marketing. She worked part time for the dean of her college and was a member of several clubs and president of her sorority. She graduated in 2005 without having any student loans, thanks to grandpa. After graduation, she was hired by Aramark in Chicago as a human resources director for Northwest Jewish Hospital. There she met Jake who was also working for that firm. Jake, an only child, was born and raised in Decatur, Illinois, where his mother, Christine still lives.

Amy and Jake dated for a few years and got married on September 13, 2008 at a winery in Hollister, California. Norma and I sponsored the rehearsal dinner in the wine storage room and a large white tent was used the following day for the dinner and dancing.

The newlyweds bought a condo in the Buck Town area of Chicago and remained there for several years before transferring to San Diego.

Amy and Jake

Daniel, Norma and me

Norma and me with all our grandchildren at that time.

Amy's brothers, Daniel and Jeffrey, were among the groomsmen, her sister Janine a bridesmaid, cousins Molli flower girl and Sammy the ring bearer

Joel and Amy

Norma, Amy and Werner

Amy received her master's degree online in human resources management. She graduated in 18 months in June 2010 while continuing to work full-time at Aramark. She and Jake both transferred to San Diego for several years and Amy received a major promotion to human resources director for Aramark for all the Chicago schools and they returned to Chicago.

They had a baby girl, Emerson Lee, on October 29, 2016, our first great grandchild.

Werner, Norma and Emerson Lee 11/29/16

Chapter 44
Marsi, Chayim's Family and Wedding

After attending San Diego State and then Northridge College for too many years, I informed Marsi it was time to graduate, and she did. She worked part-time at a bank while attending Northridge.

After graduation, she got a job at a real estate office that handled rent-controlled apartments in Santa Monica.

One morning a young man came in to inquire about renting an apartment, and the front desk manager helped him fill out the forms. A short time after leaving he called and asked if he could talk to the girl with the dark hair sitting at the back desk. He was informed of his approval to rent an apartment, and then transferred to the girl with the dark hair.

They spoke for 20 minutes and set a date for the following week. That was our daughter, Marsi, and the young man was Chayim Frenkel, the Cantor at Kehillat Israel, a Reconstructionist Congregation, in Pacific Palisades.

That afternoon, Marsi received a bouquet of long stem red roses from him. After their first date, she called us late in the evening to tell us she found the man she was going to marry.

Chayim's father, Uri*, was also a Cantor. He was born in Munkatch Czechoslovakia to an orthodox family. Uri ran away from home at the age of 10 and survived in Europe by dancing and singing in taverns in exchange for food and lodging. He eventually made his way to Leeds England where a loving family took him in. In Leeds, Uri studied and became a Chazzan. From Leeds he traveled to Pittsburgh, where he made his home and became a beloved cantor.

Sari, a holocaust survivor, originally from Koshetza, Czechoslovakia, was living in Montreal. Sari was invited by a cousin to Pittsburgh with the intention of introducing her to Uri. After a short courtship, they were married. Their two eldest children, Tzvi* (of blessed memory) and Mira were born in Pittsburgh. They moved for a short time to Phoenix Arizona and then in the 1950's to Los Angeles. In 1961 Chayim was born.

Sari and her best friend Panina started Balabusta Caterers. Sari and Uri hosted a gala engagement party for Marsi and Chayim catered by Balabuste, in December 1988 at Temple Mariv in Encino where Uri was the Cantor. Judy, Sari's sister, Uncle Abe, their children and grandchildren from Montreal, Canada all came to celebrate.

*Uri was the technical director, performed and coached Neil Diamond in the movie "The Jazz Singer." Chayim was also in some scenes in the movie.

The Balabusta's catered the hors d'oeuvre, the likes of which were unbelievable, food for the bedecking, ketubah signing and dinner after the wedding ceremony.

Norma, sons Joel & Ted, Marsi, Werner, son Bob, March 18, 1989

Werner, Norma, Marsi, Grandma Paula, Norma's mother, Chayim, his parents, Sari and Uri

Chayim and brother Ztvi* and sister Mira

Chayim and Marsi's eldest daughter, Mandi Alexis, was born on August 19, 1992, the same day as Uri. We all enjoyed celebrating their birthdays together until Mandi was three years old.

As a baby in her car seat, Mandi was always singing. She has a marvelous voice and started singing solo at the high holy days services when she was eight years old. She continued with Chayim and the choir until she was a teenager, when she chose to become orthodox. She then started going to services where many of her religious relatives from her father's side belonged. She performed in plays at YULA, the orthodox high school she attended, as well as other stage productions. She is greatly missed at KI's

*Ztvi passed away in 1992 at the age of 39 from a rare bacterial infection.

195

high holiday services. We have many CDs of her singing at the services, and recordings of her and Chayim.

Molli Henni, named after my mother, was born on January 22, 2001.She and Mandi are our fifth and sixth grandchildren.

oppy and Nanny holding their Frenkel grandchildren: Mandi and Molli

Marsi,Chayim, Molli, Mandi in Israrel

Mandi, in the stage production of Oklahoma.

Molli and Mandi in Israel

Marsi, Chayim and Molli in Israel

L-Marsi, Chayim and Molli in Israel at Molli's Bat Mitzvah. R- The party in LA 2015

The family loves going to Israel. Mandi became an Israeli citizen in 2015.

Chapter 45
OSE Reunion March 25-26, 1989

On March 25, 1989, at B'Nai David Judea
Congregation in Los Angeles, there was a 50th
anniversary dinner celebration for all the OSE children
who came from Europe to the United States. The
following day there was a brunch hosted by Fred and
Margareta Jammer and Henry and Anita Schuster.

The reunion committee included OSE alumni now
living in the Los Angeles area, including:

Morris and Renee Eisenberg, Eric and Eileen
Greene, Fred and Margareta Jammer, Aaron (master of
ceremonies) and Ellie Low, Art and Trudie Kerns,
Norbert and Marion Rosenblum, Henry and Anita
Schuster, most of whom I knew from Europe or from
the many get-togethers at Art and Trudie's home.

At the reunion there were 70 OSE alumni children
from all over the country and the world, with their
spouses and children, for a total of 260 people. Most of
us were originally from Germany, Vienna, and Poland,
and went to France between 1939 and 1940, all while
we were cared for by OSE.

One by one we each spoke to the entire assembly
about the orphanage we had lived in while in France
and what we had done since coming to the United
States. Jack Hirsch and his wife Gladys came from

Atlanta, Jack's brother, Rabbi Asher Hirsh, came from Israel, and their sister Flora from Corona, California where she had been the town mayor. Elfriede Schloss and her husband Ed came from Chicago. They now live in San Diego.Eva Kugler came from New York and now lives in London.

Eva and her mother, Mia Amalia Kanner, who was a cook at Montintin, wrote a very interesting book about their families' lives'. *Shattered Crystals*, as told to Eva by her mother, is the story of Eva's life in Germany and France and the years that followed. To access the book, go to http://shatteredcrystals.net

There was a large display of pictures and memorabilia to see. It was an emotional evening seeing people for the first time after 50 years, reminiscing with them as well as hearing all their stories. Most of the adults from the group were older than me and had more history to share.

The OSE alumni were given a questionnaire. Eva Kugler, who lived with me at Montintin in 1940-41, collected the surveys, then interviewed many of us, compiled all the information, and made it available to all. Eva was the same age (10) as I was and came to the United States on the second transport in September 1941.

BEFORE AND AFTER — Above: In 1939, Jacob Hirsch, Anselm Hirsch and Oswald Kernberg, from left, posed outside a home for refugee children near Paris. Below: Fifty years later the three line up in the same order as Jack Hirsch, Rabbi Asher Hirsch and Arthur Kern.

L-R: Jack Hirsch, Anselm Hirsch and Art Kerns
1939 and 1989*

These are some of the results of the survey: many changed their names; Ernst became Ernest, Jakob became Jack, Julius became Jay, Inge became Jane, Eugen became Gene, Helmut became Harvey, Manford, Siefried and Fritz all became Fred, Hanns and Heinz became Henry, Oswald Kernberg became Art Kern.

*All three have passed away.

The largest number of the children settled in New York and California.

There were many stories from the children who lived in foster homes, some having lived in 1, 2, 3 and even 5 different ones. The overall tone was that there was very little love, if any in most. Some foster parents were paid to foster a child and the money was their main motive.

Some children who stayed in orphanages their entire time fared better than some who went to foster homes.

In spite of our traumatic childhoods, most of the adults surveyed went on to live productive lives, married, and raised a family. None of us ever became a burden on the United States and many, including myself, served in the U.S. armed services. At least half obtained college degrees and became medical doctors, attorneys, engineers, college professors, business owners, or pursued other professions.

After reading about some of the experiences that happened in foster homes, I consider myself fortunate for having lived on a ranch. Some foster children had to work in the family business to earn their keep.

Yes, I worked at the ranch but I did it because I enjoyed doing it.

Chapter 46-A Man for All Seasons

I became a Mason on August 2, 1965 and in 2015 I celebrated 50 years of being a member of this organization.

In June of 1991, I was reading the San Diego Union-Tribune classified section and noticed an ad for a one-week volunteer counselor position for the YMCA, Camp Stepping Stone for handicapped children. I called and was informed the camp was in the Laguna Mountains, a one-hour drive east of San Diego. I applied and was accepted. I had never been to such a camp nor had I served as a counselor and thought it would be a great to be a part of an incredibly worthwhile endeavor.

There were six boys in each cabin with bunk beds that had to be kept clean and orderly, with inspection every morning (ours always got the top rating.) and a community mess hall for all the campers and staff. Only one of my six boys, Isaac, was in a wheelchair.

The camp had a lake, swimming pool, and lots of rustic cabins. The weather was great for the entire week. During the day, all the campers enjoyed swimming, horseback riding, canoeing, archery, fishing, arts and crafts and having time to write a letter home. In the evening we sat around campfires and sang. Every boy in my group participated in all events. Isaac was a real trooper. It was always so rewarding to see him horseback riding, to help him in the swimming pool or to see any of the kids catching a fish.

All the other counselors were young adults. I was the only senior counselor (60 years old) and will never forget the joy and happiness on the faces of the kids during the many activities. At the end of the week, honors were given to the staff.
I received the award for:

Outstanding achievements in "being the most enthusiastic camp counselor Camp Marston YMCA has ever seen.

L- All campers, me on far left   R- My six boys & me

October 14, 2013

Mr. and Mrs. Werner Dreifuss
6095 Caminito Pan
San Diego, CA 92120

Dear Norma and Werner,

We are very grateful for your continued involvement with Seacrest Village Retirement Communities and your most generous support of our Capital Campaign. We would not be where we are today without your commitment.

Enclosed is a statement regarding your gift to the Seacrest Foundation to support the expansion project of Seacrest Village Retirement Communities.

We thank you for your continued support and generosity and in making a difference in the lives of our current and future residents.

With best regards to you both,

Melanie Hoff

Melanie Hoff
Associate Director of Philanthropy

Enc.

For many years, Norma and I have been active supporters of Seacrest Village, the Jewish retirement home. I served on the board of trustees from 2006 to 2009, however, due to our extensive amount of travel and time spent away from home, I felt the position needed to be filled by someone with more time to devote to Seacrest. Norma and I continues to serve on the committee for the annual fundraiser dinner.

CITY OF HOPE EXTENDS SPECIAL APPRECIATION TO

Werner Dreifuss & Norma Dreifuss

*for ten or more years of unfailing dedication and loyalty to City of Hope in
the fight against cancer, diabetes and other serious diseases.*

Alexandra M. Levine, M.D., M.A.C.P.
Chief Medical Officer

There is always Hope

Approximately nine years ago my son-in-law, Cantor Chayim Frenkel, invited me to a basketball game. It was the Tel Aviv Maccabees and the Los Angeles Clippers playing at Staples Center in Los Angeles. The evening was a fundraiser for Migdal Ohr and Chayim was singing the National Anthem, so course I accepted the invitation. I was amazed and so happy to see a packed house. Several nights before, the Maccabees played the New York Knicks at Madison Square Garden. Sponsoring two such events is remarkable and speaks volumes for Migdal Ohr, the largest Jewish orphanage in the world, located in northern Israel. Until this evening I had never heard of this organization.

The person responsible for starting and sustaining the orphanage, Rabbi Grossman, was sitting on the bench with the Israeli players, wearing traditional orthodox garb including the black hat and black suit. Chayim and I had front row seats near the bench and during halftime I had a chance to speak with the Rabbi.

This was the beginning of my relationship with Migdal Ohr.

Every two years Chayim and Marsi lead a two-week family tour from Kehillat Israel Synagogue, (KI), to Israel. July 14, 2010, Norma and I decided to go to Israel on our own but join KI's tour intermittently. We had been to Israel several times and had our own agenda for this trip.

One thing Norma and I wanted to do while in Jerusalem was to visit the Hebrew University, Mount Scopus Campus. This is where our friends, Linda and Michael Bennett's daughter, Marla, and eight others were murdered by a bomb that was set off in a café on campus.

The cab driver who drove us to the university happened to be the nephew of the manager of the café who was away at the time of the explosion.

Our public relations guide informed us that a ceremony commemorating the eighth anniversary of the terrorist attack was scheduled for the following day and we attended.

Our other interest in going was to visit Migdal Ohr, "The Tower of Light". I had gone to their web site, www.Migdalohr.org, many times but I felt the need to physically see the facility. I also wanted Chayim, Marsi, their girls Mandi and Molli. and our oldest grandson, Daniel, who was in Israel at that time, to visit and see for themselves what Rabbi Grossman had built.

When we arrived a staff member, who we thought would be our guide, welcomed us. We were escorted to the Rabbi's very modest office for some light refreshment and cold drinks, a real treat on a hot summer day.

Then, unexpectedly, Rabbi Grossman came into the room, was introduced to us and then sat down and joined our family. He went on about the history of

Migdal Ohr. As a young Rabbi, 7th generation Israeli born, he was sent to Ha'Emek to rehabilitate the young adult Jews who were in the discos, jails, etc. He became known as the "Disco Rabbi".

Rabbi Grossman, Chayim, Norma, me, Daniel, Molli, Mandi & Marsi

AFMO Executive Vice President Robert Katz, West Coast Advisory mittee Chair Mitch Julis and Rabbi Grossman present a special thank you Norma and Werner Dreifuss of San Diego (L-R)

Whoever saves a Jewish soul it is as if they have saved an entire world

Sanhedrin Chapter 4,
Mishna 5

Certificate of Appreciation

To our dear friends,

Werner and Norma Dreifuss

Please accept this certificate in recognition of and appreciation for your genuine concern for the children of Israel.

Your donation supporting 12 children as part of the "Adopt-a-Child" project will allow us to provide these children with a warm home in a loving environment and will present these children with the opportunity for a successful future.

May you continue to do true acts of chesed and may you be blessed with much health, happiness and success in the future.

Sincerely yours,

Rabbi Yitzchak Dovid Grossmann

209

Sometime later a very poor Jewish family requested that Rabbi and his wife take their five children and care for them. This was the beginning of Migdal Ohr.

Today, it is a 65-acre campus housing 1,500 living on the premises and more than 6500 Jewish children from infants to young adults are cared for and educated. From one central kitchen over 15,000 meals a day are served. They have a staff of over 800, 70% percent are alumni of Migdal Ohr. The woman who served us refreshments was an alumnus and had been working there for over 30 years. The orphanage has sister schools and youth facilities throughout Israel.

Rabbi Grossman had been offered the position of Chief Rabbi of Israel twice but refused, as Migdal Ohr is his main passion. After finishing our refreshments, Rabbi Grossman invited us to accompany him to visit the kids in their classrooms and to tour the campus. Gifts had been collected and we handed them out to more than 300 girls. There is a nursery for infants and a preschool, both of which were having naptime. Many of the buildings had the names of donors, mainly people from Los Angeles and New York. There is even a bridal shop housed in what was the Rabbi's original home. Everything a bride needs is provided free of charge. The tour of the facility took several hours after which we stayed for lunch in the Rabbi's office. Migdal Ohr is a magnificent and magical operation.

The Israeli government partially subsidizes the organization and donations do the rest. There is American Friends of Migdal Ohr located in New York. Visit www.Migdalohrusa.org. Supporting a child at the orphanage greatly contributes to building the children's pride and love for of Israel.

A staff photographer followed us the entire stay and when we arrived home we received a lovely photo album with all the pictures.

Pictures from Migdal Ohr

Chapter 47
Never a Dull Moment at Our Store

When Joel, who was familiar with the operation, came back to San Diego in 1983 and joined me in working at our store, the landscape of merchandising was undergoing major changes.

The big box and discount stores were rapidly coming on the scene and encroaching on all areas including North Park. They were selling items similar to ours such as jeans, shorts, jackets, underwear, shoes, boots, sweats, socks and everything else under the sun.

All of our new mopeds had been sold. The gas shortage was over and fuel prices were back to normal. We were still buying and selling used mopeds, but slowly phasing out that part of the business.

It was never a dull at the store. I bought a tremendous variety of items including boxed Christmas and general greeting cards, plastic Christmas trees, pool tables, talking Bibles, large size family Bibles, small Yamaha organs, auto seat covers, furniture, Youngstown kitchens, appliances, paint, formal dresses, men's suits, sport coats, slacks, London Fog raincoats, jeans, men's and ladies shoes, infants/toddlers' clothes, and stationery, just to mention a few. I also bought out many businesses, held sales at their locations and then moved the remaining inventory to our store. It didn't matter what it was, if I could see making a buck, I'd buy it.

Our wives usually came with us on our buying trips twice a year at the Surplus Dealers Trade Show in Las Vegas. We started buying new and surplus military items from dealers and manufacturers from all over the US and the world. We also started buying military items from individuals and since then have continued doing so.

Early in the morning before the show opened, the major military surplus dealers would stage a fashion show, strictly with military items. One year we brought Amy, Joel's one year-old daughter with us. She had just started walking, and she opened the fashion show by toddling across the stage wearing a woodland camouflage fatigue outfit that we had brought from our store. She was a big hit and was on the front page of the following month's Army-Navy magazine, Associated Surplus Dealers magazine and other affiliated magazines.

Times were always exciting at the store with all the East/West German and Russian uniforms, boots, folding shovels and backpacks coming on the market. American camouflage uniforms were constantly changing. The many conflicts in Vietnam and in the Mideast propelled our business. Special units from the US Navy, who had received their assignments, needed special uniforms and we could and would supply them faster than their Navy supply offices.

All natural or disasters caused by human beings, oil spills from tankers or wells, to terrorist attacks all over the world or US, affected our business. Many workers from San Diego needed special clothing for their jobs, like coveralls, heavy jackets, jeans, rubber and regular boots, thermal underwear, wool socks, caps, scarves and gloves, raingear, duffle bags and backpacks.

September 25, 1978 was a very sad day as PSA flight 182 and a Cessna collided over North Park killing 144 people, 135 on PSA, 2 on the Cessna and 7 on the ground. Twenty-two homes were destroyed or damaged. I was in my office in the back of our store just before opening. The building shook and there was a very loud boom. I rushed out and saw silver pieces from the planes coming down and a large black cloud of smoke rising just a few blocks south.

Y2K was another boost in business for us. People thought the world was coming to an end. We couldn't keep up with demand for gas masks, meals ready to eat (MREs), 55-gallon and smaller water containers, water purification pumps and tablets, hand-cranked portable radios, cots, wool military blankets, flashlights, water proof matches, etc.

We had bought about 1000 new Israeli gas masks from a dealer north of Sacramento who we had been doing business with for many years, but he wasn't shipping them. I think he wanted to sell them at a higher price than the low price we had agreed upon. The price for masks was going up by the hour.

I flew up to Sacramento with Norma, rented a U-Haul truck, checked into a motel and early the next morning drove to his warehouse and demanded the masks. Within half an hour, all the masks plus a few other items were loaded and we were on our way back to the store. Norma was on the phone checking with other dealers along the way for more gas masks. There was nothing available. All this took place during the hot summer and while driving through central California, the air conditioner quit. We just put the windows down, put wet towels on our heads, drank gallons of cold drinks and drove up to our warehouse next to the store, about 9:30 that night. It was roughly a 575-mile drive and was quite an experience, like doing the *Cannonball Run*. The following day, we simply let the customers pick the gas masks from the shipping boxes, many of which had been pre-sold to them the day before.

During many of these historical events, the local and national newspapers, and radio and TV station reporters were at our store to write stories, as well as broadcast directly about the latest news, the effect it was having on our business and what kind of merchandise the costumers were buying. It was great free advertising.

One of our good customers was Stu Segall Productions, based in San Diego. They filmed many TV series and movies including *Silk Stockings* and *Rising Sun*, for which they rented our store for an entire day to shoot a segment. Two blocks were completely cornered off for all their trucks with filming equipment, props, costumes, changing rooms, makeup rooms, as well as a commissary to feed the 150 workers and actors. At the end of filming, they all started buying items in the store. They also filmed the TV series, *Pensacola: Wings of Gold* starring James Brolin, Barbara Streisand's husband. The uniforms and props were purchased from us. The series was on television for 3 years, from 1997 to 2000.

A few days before Christmas we got a call from Stu Segall production asking if we could get them 135 new military-issue flight jackets to give as presents to their staff and actors. The fact that they wanted them "now" which required overnight shipping at an additional cost of about $25 each didn't matter. We had them in our store the following morning.

One day I was at the cash register, located near the front of the store, and in walks the former president of the United States, Jimmy Carter, his wife Rosalynn, and several plain-clothes secret service men. We had not been informed of their visit. I was very surprised and for the moment didn't know how to address him. I simply said, "Hello Mr. Carter" and we shook hands.

L-R Joel Dreifuss, Rosalynn Carter, former US president Jimmy Carter and Werner June 23, 1990

The Carters were in Mexico for Habitat for Humanity International. They were on their way to Alaska to do a documentary and Rosalynn needed some boots and somebody had recommended our store.

Joel helped her try on boots; she found two pairs and purchased both. In the meantime, I was showing Jimmy all around the store. He was very pleasant and low-key and said that he wished there was a store like ours in his hometown. I asked him if he would mind if we all took a picture together. He said they would be glad to.

The local playhouses, and the Follies in Palm Springs bought uniforms and props for many of their productions.

Dollywood in Tennessee bought some tall 18-inch brown lace-up women's boots many years ago. One of our boot suppliers must have recommended us.

Chapter 48-The German Connection

Norma's cousin, Hal Mishkin, and his wife Barbara owned and operated the Pacific Crest Motel in Santa Barbara, California, for many years.

One of their frequent guests was the Kaestle family: Gisela, her husband, Yorim, and son Oliver (Olli) from Cologne, Germany. They returned to the motel almost every summer and became very good friends with the Mishkins. One year, Gisela and Olli came without Yorim, who had passed away at age 39. He had worked for the German government on Atomic Projects.

On many occasions during the years, Hal had told us about the Kaestle familly and suggested I meet them. It finally happened at Hal and Barbara's son Greg's (our daughter's twin cousin) wedding on October 10, 1999 in Santa Barbara.

Gisela is a tall slim woman who speaks English very well and who worked at a bank in Berg Gladback near her home about 30 minutes from Cologne in Germany. She told me that she was born in Darmstadt, Germany where I thought I was born, and where her mother and sister still lived.

She and her mother played in ping-pong competitions all over the world in their respective age divisions for many years.

One of her aunts had bought a department store, where she had worked, from the Jewish owner who left before the war, on the condition that he could buy

Gisela

it back if he ever returned, which never happened. According to Gisela, who worked there as a teenager, the store was destroyed during the bombings and her family physically rebuilt it brick by brick.

Gisela insisted that Norma and I come to Germany and stay with her, which Hal and Barbara had done several times, to help me try to find any records of my family.

She and her son, Olli, now grown and was married at that time, and his in-laws, assured us that would be well taken care of and we would see a very different Germany. I had never intended to return to Germany and told her that sometime in the future, if the time was right, we might visit.

221

Chapter 49-Visiting Ted in Zurich

In 1998, Ted, our youngest son, was still working for the orthodontic supply company in Orange County that recruited him from college. He had been promoted to vice president of European operations. His headquarters were in Zurich, Switzerland and he was responsible for setting up a sales force throughout Europe.

At the end of one of our cruises in the Mediterranean, we flew to Zurich, where we had never been, to visit Ted. The entire city was inundated with hundreds of life-size plastic cows on the streets, the squares, in front of and in the display windows of stores, on top of store overhangs, and hanging from the ceiling in the train station. They were standing in various positions, lying down, sitting and painted with stripes, and everything else imaginable.

We only saw one bull. When we went back the next day to take a picture, it was gone. Someone had stolen it. It was the most fascinating advertising theme I'd ever seen. When the promotion ended I was told many of them were auctioned with the funds going to charity.

Norma and I even visited a military surplus store. The owner had bought some items from our store when he was in San Diego. He was surprised and happy to see us. Ted showed us all the sites of interest, and it was really fun and very interesting. He lived there for several years and then his company bought a dental supply business headquartered in Amsterdam and he moved there.

Moo Moo here, Moo Moo there, Moo Moo everywhere

Chapter 50
Ted & Niki, the Courtship

Ted moved to Laren, a small village a few miles from Amsterdam in 1998.

In early December, he was shopping for household items at a local store, and the following occurred as per Niki:

I met Ted early December 1998 at a store, beds and bedding on a Saturday, both shopping for 'household' items in a small village called Laren. We liked each other as Americans right away, or at least I did.

He was wearing sweats and a baseball cap. We did the usual expat exchange, what are you doing here? Where are you from? Etc.

We said good-bye and stated that we should get together sometime soon.

My phone rang 20 minutes later, "Want to have dinner tonight?"

It was just a couple hours away. I got nervous, but said yes and that I would meet him somewhere. He was an exciting stranger to me and I didn't want him picking me up at my home. I also soon learned that I liked this man.

We had an incredible first date and afterwards spent much time exploring the villages of Europe, took multiple ski trips and visits to Monte Carlo.

Chapter 51-Niki and Family

Niki was born in London on October 25, 1968. Her mother Helen was born in Limavady, Northern Ireland in April 1946, and her family moved to London when she was young. Helen's father was a chef and even baked birthday cakes for the queen.

Niki's father, William Wayne Hodges, was an enlisted man in the US Air Force, stationed at Chicksands AFB, just outside of London. He met Helen at a typical British pub.

They married a year later and moved to Panama City, Florida where Wayne had been transferred when Niki was 6 weeks old. Her brother, Ian, was born 18 months later.

After Wayne's discharge, he attended the University of Florida. After graduation, he went to officer candidate school and then pilot training in Lubbock, Texas, where Niki's sister, Wendi, was born in 1976. Niki's family was constantly moving, as was life with a pilot and career officer.

Her parents divorced in 1988, and Helen remained in Washington, D.C. Her father remarried shortly after, had triplets and retired 20-some years later as two-star general. His last assignment was at the Pentagon.

In 1987, Niki graduated from Doherty High School in Colorado Springs, where I was stationed while in the

Army in 1955, and in 1992 with a bachelor's degree from American University in Washington, D.C.

She met Fabrice Francois in college and married him in 1993 in Bethesda, MD. They moved to Boston in the fall of 1994 where Niki was an event planner for Reebok for three years.

Fabrice passed away in July of 1996. He was struck by a hit and run driver while walking in the neighborhood on a 4th of July weekend.

Niki remained in the Boston area for a year and a half after his death, then in the summer of 1998 she moved to the Netherlands to begin working as an event planner for Nike.

Top left: Werner/Ted, middle: Ted/Niki and Werner/Norma at Ted's birthday party 2000 Right, Ted holding 3 month-old Baron, a Great Dane

Chapter 52
Ted and Niki's Wedding

Ted and Niki set their wedding day for July 14, 2001, Bastille Day, a major French holiday. The ceremony was in the beautiful Loire Valley, Tours, Chateau Amboise, in southern France.

Niki studied in southern France while in college, and she and Ted had visited there several times.

This was marvelous for many reasons. Niki would be a great addition to our new family and also this would give Norma and me a reason to return to Europe and accept Gisela's offer to visit Germany.

Niki arranged for her mother, Helen, to meet at the Royal Hotel in Paris, just a block from the Arc de Triumph, and then drive together with us to Tours. She also made all the hotel reservations in Tours.

Norma booked the flights and arranged a car for us to pick up in Paris and drop off in Germany.

We notified Gisela of our plans. She was delighted and used part of her vacation time from the bank to coincide with our visit.

We flew into Paris a few days before we were to meet Ted, Niki and her mother to go visit the orphanage in Eaubonne where I had lived in 1940. The second day we did some sightseeing in Paris, including going to the top of the Eiffel Tower, which I remember seeing as a young boy in 1939, and taking a boat ride on the Seine River.

The third day we were coming down in the hotel elevator with another woman and I said, "You're Niki's mother," whom we had never met. In amazement she said, "Yes, how did you know?" "Just premonition," I said.

Ted and Niki also arrived that day. Niki, her maid of honor, Judith Parker, and several other girls had a night out as did Ted with his best man and several others.

The next day, we picked up our car, a Volvo station wagon, just like one that Niki had in Holland. Niki drove the Volvo to Tours with her mother and Norma, following Ted, with an English speaking GPS, and me. It was the first time I ever encountered a GPS, which was located in his trunk on a CD.

Bob, our middle son, Sheppy, (Hal's younger brother and Norma's cousin,) who was living in Amsterdam, and our daughter, Marsi arrived the next day. Marsi's youngest daughter, Molli, just five months old stayed home with her daddy.

Several of Niki's aunts and uncles from her mother's side drove from England to the wedding.

Our hotel near Tours

Chateau de Rochecotte was at one-time the residence of Prince de Talleyrand and had been converted into a beautiful boutique hotel. The main building was very similar in construction to the orphanage in Eaubonne.

I asked the front desk clerk if it was possible for me to see their wine cellar. She immediately summoned a person to take me. Just as I had surmised, it had the same musty odor as the air raid shelter "wine cellar" at the orphanage in Eaubonne. My next request was if I could have my wife and three children (Bob, Ted and Marsi) also visit the wine cellar. I wanted them, if possible, to transcend and possibly connect in some small way to my childhood and the time I spent in the musty air raid shelter. And it came to be. Other members of the wedding party also accompanied them but had absolutely no idea whatsoever why I had made the arrangement.

229

On Friday July 13, 2001, at an old castle, Norma and I hosted a prenuptial dinner party for family and the wedding party. The ambiance, food, and wines were outstanding. The entire setting was like a fairytale.

Romantic Ted presented Niki with diamond earrings, and for those from out of town to witness, on one knee he proposed to her all over again.

July 14th, the day of the wedding, began with torrential rains, and all the public fireworks for that night were canceled. Fortunately, the rain stopped at noon, the sun dried out the gardens at the Chateau D'Amboise and the wedding took place outside as planned.

A Rabbi from Paris performed the ceremony. Niki's father walked her down the path and Norma and I walked Ted down.

A cocktail reception for the 44 guests followed in the gardens, from which we had the most spectacular view of the Loire Valley and river below.

Dining and dancing was in the Chateau D'Amboise, which was built in the 15th and 16th centuries by Charles VIII, Louis XII and Francois I, and where Leonardo da Vinci lived out his last years. It is now a museum filled with furniture from that era. For the wedding reception everything was moved to the sides of the room and a kitchen was set up outside. It was spectacular and lasted into the wee hours of the night.

Niki, her father, Wayne and Marsi on left taking picture

Werner, Ted, and Norma

Ted and Niki

The Chateau D'Amboise and garden cocktails
reception

L-R Charles Elkouby, best man, Judith Parker, maid of honor, Werner, Norma, Ted, Niki, her mother Helen Hodges, her father Wayne Hodges, Bobby and Marsi.

Niki and Ted left one day after the wedding to the British West Indies to enjoy their honeymoon. For their marriage to become legal in the eyes of the U.S. they married again, in white, on the beach, in front of a Baptist Minister.

L-R Norma, Werner, Niki, Ted, Judith and Wayne
Hodges and Helen

Several days after the wedding, Norma, our son
Bob, Norma's cousin Sheppy and I drove south to
Limoges and Montintin, the orphanage as described
earlier.

It is now a gated area and the owner wouldn't allow
us in to visit. We spent a night in town and the
following day had the local tourism office call to
attempt to get us in, but to no avail. From there we
headed to the coast and on to Normandy. Bob did the
driving through many picturesque villages, where we
would always find signs on the corners indicating the
ratings of the small hotels for the night's lodging.

234

Chapter 53-Normandy

We continued on to Normandy and Omaha Beach where the Allied invasion of Europe took place in 1945. It was early in the morning; hardly any visitors and the weather could not have been more perfect with bright sun and clear blue sky.

One of Leah Shapov's cousins, Herman Addleson, who I knew, and was loved by all who knew him, was a proud US Army paratrooper. He was one of the thousands killed during the invasion. He was one of nine children, never married and many of his nieces and nephews still live in San Diego and are friends Norma's and mine.

It was an eerie feeling walking along the silent deserted beach with only a large monument commemorating the invasion, and the remains of the German bunkers above overlooking us.

After getting a plot plan at the office indicating Herman's grave site, we made our way through the most immaculately kept grounds with thousands of perfectly straight rows of grave markers. Herman's grave marker, the Star of David, had many small stones on top indicating prior visitors. It was surrounded by many cross-markers identifying the brave souls buried there, and many reading only, "Here lay the remains only known to God."

We had an unexpected treat of the 60 members, ranging from 16 to 60 years of age, Boston Drum Fyfe Crops performing in their colorful uniforms and marching through the cemetery. They were touring Europe and just happened to be there that day. There are many large monuments depicting the European battles fought by the Allied troops. Every European who has ever bad-mouthed the United States should be required to visit Normandy and to learn about the thousands of lives America and its Allies sacrificed so others can enjoy freedom.

War is a tragic occurrence and regardless of the outcome, everyone loses. The destruction of property, but more importantly human lives, as well as the emotional, physical and psychological damage inflicted upon on both sides, takes generations to heal and recover, if ever. War is caused mainly by greed, lust for power, or territorial boundary disputes.

Upon leaving Normandy, we continued to Brussels for one night. That day happened to be a holiday and the main street was closed to auto traffic. People were dressed in all kinds of costumes and parading down the street. All the museums were open free of charge, as was a large synagogue, which had a line of people for two blocks waiting to go through it.

Of course, we had some famous Belgian waffles.

The following day we continued on almost a straight drive west to Cologne, Germany, to Gisela's. On the way, we encountered some sort of protest with tires being burned on the highway, causing us some delay.

Chapter 54-Returning to Germany

Returning to Germany was, almost like traveling to a new country for me.

It had been 62 years since I had been evacuated from Waisenhauses, the orphanage in Frankfurt, at the age of eight. Except for the orphanage, there is very little that I remembered about Germany.

One must look forward to make sure where you are going, making changes as required and make sure the past isn't repeated. There is absolutely nothing anyone can do to alter the past. It is done, gone, finished, and kaput, as it's only history. To dwell on the past is a total exercise in futility, and it will destroy you.

Gisela welcomed us with open arms to her first-floor; corner-unit home in a four-story 30-unit condo complex situated in a lovely wooded area with small lakes and walking and bicycle paths.

She had a delicious lunch waiting for us. We spent the rest of the afternoon visiting with her and her son, Olli, a tall, handsome, young man who arrived on his bicycle. We had heard about him, but never met him or his wife, who was attending medical school. He was working for a major German company, similar to GE, as well as being a member of a small band.

The following day Gisela drove Norma, Bob, Sheppy and me to Darmstadt, checked us into a hotel and then on to Gisela's sister's home where her mother also lived. The first thing, of course, was to have some of their delicious homemade sandwiches and cakes. Then we drove through the main part of town and visited Gisela's aunt at her department store that is operated by her nephew. The multi-floor store was purchased from the original Jewish owner before the war, destroyed by the Allied bombings, and rebuilt by her aunt's family after the war.

We went to the city hall to check records, trying to find any information about my family, but there was nothing. The Allied bombings in World War II had destroyed most of the town, including most of the records.

Gisela's aunt knew the person in charge of a beautiful new synagogue that had been built by the German government and she arranged for us to tour it with hopes of finding some records there, but to no avail. The synagogue has 160 families as members, mostly from Russia, with a kosher social hall and kitchen, schoolrooms and a very modern sanctuary. The following day we returned to Gisela's home and met Olli's in-laws, Granada and Theo, who is a retired college professor and an avid gardener. He took care of Gisela's small, lovely, backyard.

When he was a young boy, Theo's parents sent him to a farm to keep him from having to join the Brown Shirt Nazi Youth.

They also own a beautiful ten-acre forest that is located about an hour and half away by car. Theo knew when each and every tree was planted. He had handicapped children come at Christmas time to select trees for themselves free of charge. There was also a split log table and benches where we enjoyed Granada's homemade cakes and tea on her best china she had brought with her.

One day Gisela had to work and Theo took Norma, Bob, Sheppy and me to Cologne on the train. Theo knew every Jewish landmark including the Memorial for the Jewish victims of the Holocaust, a Jewish cemetery, and museum.

We had lunch across from the famous cathedral that is one of the few sites I remembered. Theo said he couldn't join us since he had something important to do. When I asked for the bill, I was told it already had been paid. When Theo returned, I asked for the bill, but he wouldn't hear of it.

Me, Norma, Bob and Sheppy in Cologne, Germany
2001

There was an old Mikvah, where Jewish women
bathe before getting married, located in front of the city
hall that could only be seen through a glass covered top.
It was about 30 feet below. Theo knew who had the
key, and while we had lunch, he obtained it and then
took us inside to the bottom.

Olli and his wife* had tickets to see Mark Knopfler
at the Cologne arena on July 23rd which they had
purchased a year earlier. Gisela asked if we would like
to try buying tickets on the street and join them. There
were many people trying to sell tickets at high prices.
We walked away but after the concert started the sellers
began chasing us. The prices had dropped below the
original cost at the box office. At this point I bought
them and we enjoyed the great show.
* They divorced a few years ago.

The following night we had a delicious dinner at Olli's and his wife's condo, which he prepared. Olli he gave us a CD that he made of the entire concert, which we still enjoy.

We had breakfast and dinner at Theo* and Granada's as well as many dinners at beer gardens. They all couldn't do enough for us, and it was a fabulous experience.

I gave Gisela power of attorney to try to find any records of my family. Just on a hunch, she checked the records in Frankfurt and found my birth certificate. Being born in Frankfurt entitled me to come back for two weeks with my wife, all expenses paid, for a visit, courtesy of the city. Most major cities in Germany have the same program.

Gisela contacted them and several months after, we received an invitation to visit that summer, flying on Lufthansa to Frankfurt. I asked Gisela to call them to try to change the fight for a week earlier, which she did and we had another great week visiting with her, Olli and his wife and her parents.

*Theo passed away in 2015.

Chapter 55
Our Third Dreifuss Grandson

Ted and Niki remained in Laren for about one year and then moved north to Weesp, which was closer to Amsterdam.

After another one of our cruises, Norma and I visited them for about a week. The house they leased in Weesp, a lovely small town, was very unique. It was over 100 years old, three floors on the left side with a living room on the first and a very narrow spiral staircase to bedrooms on the second and third floor, where we stayed, overlooking the backyard and a canal. It all had been renovated. The right side had originally been a stable. It was converted into a large dining room with a large passageway in the middle that had originally been the entry to the stable.

When we got to our room, there was a Teddy bear on the rocking chair with a card welcoming us and announcing the upcoming arrival of a new "baby bear" due seven months later. That was great and very exciting news.

There was a canal at the end of the backyard where Ted kept his boat. I lounged under an old weeping willow tree and watched all kinds of large yachts as well as kids on rubber rafts pass by. There was a toll bridge at the end of the block that opened for large yachts. A man with a long pole used a Dutch wooden shoe to collect the toll fee. Ted's boat fit under the bridge so he didn't have to pay.

For Ted and Niki's anniversary we went on their boat to Amsterdam for dinner at a very upscale Japanese restaurant, which is located inside a large old bakery at the Blake Hotel.

Ted notified his company of his desire to return to Orange County since his stay in Europe had extended much longer than he originally agreed to. He and Niki wanted the baby to be born in the United States. The company transferred him back, including shipping all their belongings and Baron, the Great Dane that Ted had when he met Niki and Obie, a black and white Great Dane they had bought, both the size of a Shetland pony. Special crates had to be built. They stayed in an apartment in Newport, CA until they found a house in Coto de Caza, a 5000 acre gated complex at the foot of Saddleback Mountains in Orange County. It was one level, on a cul-de sac, and had a walk-in pool with a slide. It is just 75 miles from San Diego and the same distance northwest to Marsi & Chayim's house.

On March 5, 2004, shortly after moving, Samuel Jacob Dreifuss, our 7th grandchild, was born. His uncle Chayim officiated at his Bris on March 12, my birthday. What a great present. He looked just like Ted as a baby, with lots of black hair.

Chapter 56-My New Birthday

In 2003, we booked a two-week Crystal Cruise to the Orient scheduled to depart from Singapore on March 5, 2004. On a Friday, several weeks prior to our departure, I had my usual checkup at my cardiologist's office, about 2 ½ miles from our house, close enough that usually I walked there and back.

Several years before, I woke up one morning with a cold feeling in my chest, no pain, but perspiring, as I was getting ready to go the store. I asked Norma to make me some hot tea. As usual, she never listens to me and called 911 instead. The paramedics came and took me to Alvarado Hospital, which is across the street from my cardiologist's office.

It was determined that I had a heart attack and a stent was put in. Since that time, my cardiologist, Dr. Copan's,* keeps a close eye on me.

On Monday, Norma and I went to get the results of the exam and Dr. Copans, who knew of our upcoming cruise, said that I wouldn't be going since I had what he called a "widow maker", a major blocked artery.

Since Norma wasn't ready to be a widow, I consented to have a bypass and it was scheduled for February 24 at seven o'clock in the morning.

I knew Ted and Niki had passports, having returned from Holland within the past year, so I called Ted to ask if he, Niki and Sammy would like to take our cruise, which of course they did. So Sammy celebrated his first birthday, March 5, 2004 on the day they boarded the ship.

The surgery was a 5-way bypass on February 24, my new second birthday. A vein was taken from my right leg, from which I had absolutely no pain, and was used to replace the blocked arteries.

I was in the ICU ward for a few days as was a criminal who kept everybody awake rattling his chains day and night.

When I was transferred to a private room, Marsi slept there many nights.

It seemed forever to obtain pain meds at night, and there were many nights that I wondered if it was all worth going through.

Having to sleep on my back, which I never do, was very uncomfortable, especially with all the wires attached to me. Whenever I did fall asleep, a nurse would wake me to take my blood pressure or temperature.

After a few days, I was walking down the hall with all my attachments, and I figured out how to move enough of them out of the way to sleep on my side. Marsi had a masseuse come and give me a back massage.

*Dr. Copans passed away in April 2016 of colon cancer.

After several months of therapy, or more like torture, my right shoulder healed.

I saw a shoulder doctor for my left shoulder since my hand was also in pain. He checked it over and said to just give it time to heal. I asked about my hand and he replied that he was only a shoulder doctor and I should see a hand specialist. I asked for a cortisone shot in the hand, which he did and that took care of that.

Ted, Niki and one-year-old Sammy, who had room service and a baby sitter every night, had a great cruise. Ted and Niki's names were on our place cards at the Captain's table on our following cruise.

Niki, 1 year old Sammy and Ted
2004 Crystal Serenity

Chapter 57
Celebrations and Surprises

Over the years we have enjoyed many celebrations and "surprise" parties.

For our 25th wedding anniversary, our friends Alice and Zane Feldman took Norma and me out to lunch at the Kona Kia Club on Shelter Island in San Diego. All our children, who had put together a beautiful party with many of our family and friends, surprised us.

Our children also gave us a Tauck Train Tour from Calgary, Canada to Lake Louise, Banff. We went river rafting for the first and last time, then drove over the Continental Divide in a 1923 Ford 10 passenger touring car that had been restored. We also walked on a glacier.

My 50th birthday surprise party (yes, it was a complete surprise) was held with "Playboy Bunnies" at Georgie Joe's Chinese restaurant in La Mesa on February 21st. Joel came down from Santa Cruz. There were over 100 family members and friends in attendance.

For my 60th birthday, Norma planned a "surprise party" at our condo complex clubhouse. Somehow, I knew about it and prepared a speech the night before. It was a great party. Our eight-year-old granddaughter,

Amy, greeted everyone as they entered and later she presented me with a roast. Then our four children and their spouses roasted me.

One portion was our son-in-law, Chayim, relating that one day he was at our store while I was helping a customer and what a great salesman I was. He said, "Pop sold him a fishing rod, reel, net, worms, hooks, line, and sinkers. Then an ice chest, sun hat, mosquito repellent, a boat and a trailer all totaling more than $10,000." After the man left the store, Chayim said, "Pop, how did you know that the man needed all those items?" I replied, "Well, the man came into our store looking to buy a box of Tampax for his wife which we didn't carry. So I suggested since he couldn't do anything else that weekend, he might as well go fishing."

Then Amy said a few words, followed by her brother, Daniel, ("Mr. Peepers," as we called him), who was six years old. He said, "I love Grandpa because he is very special."

We had a great 50th wedding anniversary party at the Westgate Hotel. We enjoyed their fabulous Sunday brunch with over 127 guests, three of whom came over from Europe with me, 10 members of our wedding party including our flower girl, Carole Rae, from Chicago, and a bridesmaid from New Jersey. There was a large group from my foster family, two of Sam's nieces and a group from my high school class.

Amy was in London doing an internship, and we flew her in for the celebration.

Many of Norma's out-of-town relatives came, as did Gisela from Germany.

Our son-in-law, Chayim, officiated at the wedding ceremony and asked, "Do you take this woman to be your wife?" I answered, "Can I think about that?"

We had a small band from Los Angeles and all had a great time.

It's hard to believe that was over 11 years ago. Since then, so many who attended and other acquaintances have passed away.

L-R back row Ted, Daniel, Jeffrey, Amy, me, Bob, Joel, Chayim, Middle- Niki, Norma, Janine

Front- Mandi holding 3 month old cousin Sammy, Marsi and Molli

The secret is out... I'm having an affair
with my first wife Norma, we make a great pair
We've been married 50 golden years,
through sickness and health, happiness and tears.
This anniversary means a lot to us... and so do you,
please come celebrate as we reminisce our "I do".

Sunday, June 27th
Brunch 11 am
Westgate Hotel
1055 2nd Avenue
San Diego

R.svp by June 15th.
Norma (619) 263-0276
or e-mail Nhdreifuss@aol.com

The Honor of
Your presence
is our present

Dean & Edie Greenberg, the matchmaker, Norma &
Werner

Norma is wearing a Good Conduct medal that
Amy presented her.

L-R: Werner, Al Schatz*, Norma, Marvin Zigman, and Art Kerns at our 50th anniversary party June 27, 2004

For my 75th birthday, we took Marsi and Molli (Chayim and Mandi couldn't go at that time) Ted, Niki and Sammy on a cruise from San Diego to Hawaii and back.

Niki had T-shirts and tank tops printed for all of us saying, "75 years young we love you" on the front and "Looking Good" on the back.

*Al Schatz was the husband of Irene, who was Norma's best friend in Los Angeles. Norma was the maid of honor at their wedding. Irene was matron of honor at our wedding. She passed away two weeks before our party.

Kissing cousins Molli and Sammy "the third generation"

L-R back Norma, Werner, Niki, Ted and Sammy
Front Marsi and Molli in Hawaii 2006

When we walked out from the port area in Honolulu, Chayim and Mandi were standing there holding a large sign saying "Happy birthday." Molli was so excited to see her daddy and big sister, as we all were.

It seems that we are always on a cruise during my birthday, as was the case in 2011. We were on a back-to-back cruise on the Oceana and I wanted to extend it to another segment. I asked Norma to check with the cruise consultant who told her it was all sold out. This was at the end of March.

A few days after coming home, our son, Ted, called and asked if we could babysit 7-year-old Sammy since he had to go to Hawaii early Monday on business and wanted to take Niki. Sammy is my best buddy when his mom and dad are gone, and we gladly agreed.

Ted asked if we could come Sunday since their flight was very early Monday afternoon and also to see Sammy horseback riding at the stable in their complex, Coto de Caza. When we got to the stable, Molli was there as well. Ted told us that she wanted to ride and Marsi brought her there.

I told Norma to go to Ted and Niki's house, less than ten minutes away, since she's not a great horse lover. The kids had a great time for several hours, and we left for Ted's in Niki's new van.

When we arrived, I pulled out the front seat floor mat to clean and to wipe down my boots. Ted said, "Let it go and come in the house." When we walked in, "Surprise!" People were standing all the way up the staircase holding letters spelling: HAPPY

Party time at Ted's and Niki's BIRTHDAY!   All our friends and family were there, including Norma's brother Herbie and his wife Judy, Elfriede and her husband Ed, all bussed in from San Diego. Norma's sister Carol Joy came from Los Angeles and her son Michael, wife Sharon and their daughter Sarah came from Oakland. Hal and Barbara came from Santa Barbara. Fred Simmons, one of Hy and Lil's sons and his daughters, Jill, husband and child also came.

It was remarkable that Molli and Sammy kept the party a secret while we were at the stables!

Our whole new family as of 3/26/2011
L-r back row, Jeffrey, Marsi & Chayim, Joel between WD and Jake
Second row - Bob, Molli & Sammy holding Bob's dog Daniel, Amy, Mandi, Me, Janine and Norma.
Front row Niki and Ted

Elfriede Schloss and me at my 80th birthday party

It was an all-western dude ranch theme in the house and the backyard with red bandanas that had WD printed on them, barbecue, and a western bar and music. I didn't have the slightest hint about the party, and it was great.

The biggest and best surprise came shortly after my 80th birthday party when Niki announced that she was pregnant. Sammy was already seven years old and they had given up trying to have another child.

Much to everyone's delight, on November 30, 2011 a healthy Kate (Katie) Helen Dreifuss was born, our 8th grandchild. She has been an absolute joy and when Norma and I visit, she never wants us to leave.

Husband Ed/Elfreide/ Werner at her 90th birthday party 6/2016

Kate at Big Bear Lake 2015

Kate and Sammy at Big Bear Lake 2015

Chapter 58-Return to a Stolen Past

Since the end of World War II, the city of Frankfurt am Main, as well as many other German cities, has invited former citizens to return for a two-week visit in order to try and make amends, if that's ever possible, and to see a new Germany. This was an opportunity for the survivors who were fortunate enough to have escaped the Nazi Holocaust and avoided having their names engraved on one of more than 11,000 bricks adorning the walls of the Jewish cemetery and see the new Germany.

Our invitation from Frankfurt am Main was scheduled for June 7th to June 19th, 2007. We flew in a week earlier. Olli, Gisela's son, picked us up and we spent a great week with them.

On the seventh of June, we took the bullet train to Frankfurt and met up with the other guests. We took a cab to the Hotel Frankfurt Hof, a Steigenberger Hotel which was, unbeknownst to us, only 2 blocks from the station. It was a very nice hotel in a great location, close to the Main river and a Jewish Museum.

There were 29 former Frankfurters: 21 husbands, wives, a daughter and one granddaughter, one women was from Israel, one from Sweden and the others from the United States.

We were greeted by a goup of volunteers, mostly teachers, who asked for pictures and documents so they could make copies and try to find family connections for us from prior visitors and records. They were always there to accompany us on our outings and were most helpful.

The first morning at breakfast we met a couple from Atlanta and I asked if they knew Jack Hirsch. They said they were their best friends.

The next afternoon there was a welcoming reception with the mayor of Frankfurt. She made a speech but it was in German, which I couldn't understand.

The following day, Saturday, a group of us walked to the large West End Orthodox Synagogue, which had been restored by the city. It wasn't burned down because the Germans needed the building to store the stage sets of a nearby opera house.

The street in front of the building was blocked off with a cement barrier. There was also a police Jeep with an electrical connection that is stationed there all the time with two policepersons on guard.

What does that tell you?

One member of the congregation in attendance, Hardy, was from the group that welcomed us at the hotel. They gave me an "aliyah", the honor of being called up to make a blessing from the torah and invited us all to stay for lunch.

Members of the welcoming committee took us to the Jewish Museum of Frankfurt which was just several blocks from our hotel. There we found several books that had stories and pictures, some of which I had, about Waisenhauses and our group of children.

We met one retired couple, Ellen and Larry Klien. Ellen spent half a year in New Jersey and the other half in Florida. She was born in Frankfurt. While we were all watching an old video about Frankfurt, Ellen screamed, "That's me in front!" One evening a group of us went out for dinner, and Ellen started talking to the waiter. It turns out that he had lived in the same house Ellen had lived in as a child.

One of the greeters, after seeing my pictures, mentioned there was a lady who had lived at Waisenhauses and her mother worked there. She put me in touch with Cilly Peiser, who lived in Langen, Hessen, Germany, just a half hour south of Frankfurt. I called her and made arrangements a visit at her home. Norma and I took the train, and Cilly met us at the train stop. Born October 19, 1925, she was one of the most remarkable people I have ever met, sharp as tack, and still teaching children with learning disabilities in her home. She had a temendous collection of memoribilia, about her life, Waisendhauses and the years that followed. She collected pictures, some of which I also have, books, DVD's and CDs. She spoke all over Germany in schools, churches, synagogues and general meeting places. She shared some of her life story with us. Her mother was from Czechoslovakia and her father was from Frankfurt, where they lived. Her father died leaving her mother in her early 20s with four children, the youngest, her only brother, 4 months old. She worked as a cook at Waisenhauses and was able to bring her children to live there. Cilly became friends with Elfreide, Meyer, Scholls and Henry Schuster since they were about the same age. They have stayed in touch throughout their lives.

Fast forward:

Elfreide and her husband Ed now live in San Diego and we have celebrated many happy occasions together. Henry and his wife Anita lived in Los Angeles for many years, then moved to Las Vegas and we had lunch with them a few years ago.

I am delighted that Henry lived to see his memoirs, Abraham's Son, the Making of an American published in 2010. I asked him for permission to use his book as a reference and his reply was as follows, written by his wife. Thanks Henry.

Dear Norma and Werner,

Henry asked me to write you to tell you it would be an honor if you would use any of his book. He is glad that that you are writing a book.

Henry had not been well for a number of years and passed away May 26, 2014.

When it was decided to evacuate all the childen from Waisenhauses, Queen Wilhelmina of the Netherlands invited 24 girls to come there. Cilly and only one sister were in the group that went to Holland at the end of 1938. Her older sister was sent to Israel. Her brother and mother had to stay and tragically became victims of the Holocaust.

Cilly and her sister lived in a Jewish orphange in Amsterdam and escaped the Nazi roundup of Jewish people. Because of the kindness of one German soldier they went into hiding until after the war.

Cilly immigrated to Palestine in 1946 where she married, had one daughter, divorced and returned to Germany in 1957, where she was a special education teacher. She wrote many commentaries and gave speeches about her life.

She told us she thought the German soldier who had saved her life was shot because of his kindness to the Jews. However, after returning to Germany she discovered that he was alive. She tracked him down in order to thank him. The event was recorded on DVD, *The Eye of the Needle*. I'm grateful to her for giving me a copy.

Most of the greeting staff as well as Cilly. accompanied us and took us on a cruise down the Main River.

Werner and Cilly (Levitus) Peiser on the Main
River, Frankfurt, June 20

All the guests were asked to speak at the
various schools. I volunteered to speak at a high
school, two students, a young lady and man,
picked us up at our hotel and took us to their
school via the Underground. They brought us
flowers and a box of chocolate candy.

It was a large classroom with tables arranged in
a u-shape and one in front. The kids looked like
typical American kids. I spoke in English about my
life and afterwards there was a question-and-
answer period.

One afternoon, we were taken to the oldest
Jewish German cemetery at Worme. It was a 2-
hour bus ride. The walls contained hundreds of
grave markers that the Germans used for building

roads, and there was no way to replace the markers on the correct graves after the war.

Cemetery in Worme, June 11, 2007

We were also taken to an art exhibit in a cement bunker that was built where a synagogue once stood. There were two pictures on display of Waisenhauses, one before the war, page 1, and one after the war and the Allied bombings, with the caption, Henry Schuster, Las Vegas as shown on next page.

Henry Schuster took this picture of partially destroyed Waisenhauses while stationed in Germany with the US Army after WWII 1946.

Former Waisenhauses location is now part of a large apartment building.

Over the past years, the only source of information relating to my mother's deportation was from Yad Vashem, showing her date of birth in1919, place of death, Poland and Victim's Status End WWII as Missing.

The most significant event took place on our visit to the Judisches Museum. There with the help of an employee, we found a fairly new journal containing all the names of the Holocaust victims, including my mother's. It showed that she was born in Darmstadt on November 19, 1912. Deportation 3/25/1942 to Piaski, Poland. No mention as to any further transfers.

During the German occupation of Poland during World War II, the town of Piaski became part of the semi-colonial General Government. At the beginning of this period 4,165 Jews resided in Piaski. In 1940 the Nazi German occupiers established the Piaski ghetto, to imprison not only its own Jewish inhabitants, but also several thousand Jews transported from the Lublin Ghetto, as well as from the German Reich. In 1942 the ghetto was liquidated with the use of Reserve Police Battalion 101 from Hamburg. Its inmates, loaded onto Holocaust trains, perished in the nearby Belzec extermination camp.

Fast forward:

In the spring of 2011, Norma and I were on a Oceana cruise that went into the Baltic Sea. One of the ports was Stutthof, Poland with an excursion to a

267

concentration camp in Piaski. When I tried to book it, I was informed it was all sold out. I knew that there are always a few seats left empty in case of emergencies. I told the tour director it was imperative I go. I kept on him for a few days until he finally consented to sell me two tickets. I would have gone all the way to the captain to get them. It took several hours to drive there from the port.

Not having any knowledge as to which concentration my mother was murdered, I needed to go to this one when I had the opportunity. I knew for certain I would never again return to Poland.

We toured the camp, I said Kadish, a prayer for the departed, and left the grounds.

I needed to have some closure.

Make peace with your past so it doesn't screw up your present or future.

The entrance to the camp

A memorial depicting thousands of victims' shoes

The Concentration Camp

Chapter 59-Once in a Lifetime

On March 10, 2014, we were in Singapore aboard the Crystal Serenity on our second World Cruise. There was a special dinner at the Garden City, which is a magnificent, gigantic atrium.

After the affair and picture taking, Norma and I were in a line to board the coaches. There was a beautiful lady from the ship staff on top of the stairs controlling the passenger traffic going down to the jitneys in the parking lot.

When Norma and I got to the front of the line, this lady said to me, "I need to give you a kiss and big hug," which she did, as Norma stood there in amazement. Something like that only happens once in a lifetime. Then she, the lovely Dina Sterr, told us that she was so moved when several days prior Bruce McGill, the movie actor, and guest speaker read the "Introduction to my Memoirs".

Near the end of the fifth segment on each World Cruise, staff members read three or four parts of memoirs or stories, written by guests from the memoir class taught by Joe Kita. The readings were usually held in the Avenue Saloon, which holds less than 100 people however, this year they were moved to the Stardust Lounge, which accommodates 400 guests.

Dina Sterr and her significant other for over 17 years, Kerry Millerick, are the instructors for Digital Filmmaking on the World Cruise, and their company trains and provides instructors to teach on other cruise lines. Both are extremely bright and have worked in many places in Hollywood, and with Dina producing a half time show for the Super Bowl.

Dina and Kerry also teach iPad classes in the Hollywood Theatre, which holds about 300 guests, plenty of seats since the demand for the classes are so great. I attended all their classes and even learned a few new things. We all have become very good friends.

Bridge players will appreciate this. Another once-in-a-lifetime event occurred October 1, 2015. Norma's Thursday Bridge and lunch group needed two subs for that day, so Beverly Press recruited her 91-year-old husband, Ben*, the tennis pro, joker, and our friend. Norma also recruited me. We always have a great time together so I agreed to play.

*Ben is an American tennis pro, coach, and writer, known for his involvement in World Team Tennis, his long connection with the Hotel del Coronado and for coaching San Diego tennis standout Maureen Connolly, "Little Mo," who won the Grand Slam in 1953 in her early years. Ben was a pallbearer at Maureen's funeral in 1961.

Ben was still teaching tennis at the age of 91 at the Hilton Beach and Tennis Club. He also was a member of our bridge group.

The Thursday lunch/bridge group plays and lunches at Humphries in La Jolla. When we arrived Ben says to me, "Let's bid 7 no trump when we are partners." I said, "Sure". 7 no trump can be bid usually though a series of bids but hardly ever as Ben did. When the time came and we were partners, Ben sitting north, his sister Edie (Press) Greenberg, who introduced Norma and me, sitting east, I'm sitting south and Ben's wife, Beverly, west and keeping score.

Ben opened 7 no trump, the highest bid that can be made. We all looked at him and thought he was joking. "No" he said, "that's my bid. Edie passes, I pass, having only 2-point, the jack plus 6 diamonds and jack of clubs, and Beverly passes.

He had all the aces and kings, plus the 10 of diamonds.

Ben* plays all his aces, kings and on the diamonds; the queen drops and he played his ten to my jack and runs my diamonds, making the 7 no trump.

I was delighted to bring him an early copy of this book while he was ill, which brought a big smile to his face. His response was "outstanding, super."

*Ben passed away September 9, 2016 at the age of 92.

Chapter 60-Reflection

Over the past 61 years, Norma and I have seen and been to nearly all of the most spectacular, historical, and saddest places on earth. We have traveled with our children, grandchildren, friends Ernie and Ellen Addleson, Alice and Zane Feldman, Edie and Dean Greenberg, and with Beverly and Ben Press on several Crystal Cruises. We have made hundreds of friends from all around the world. We have met so many wonderful people on our more than 75 cruises and from our temples, (Kehillat Israel,) summer trip to Israel.

Ernie & Ellen Addleson, Norma & me 1979 Alaska Princess cruise

Alice & Zane Feldman, Me & Norma in the Grand
Bazaar, Istanbul, Turkey 1998

We've stood at the top of Masada, waded in the
Dead Sea, prayed at the Wailing Wall and excavated
below the ground. We've walked the Via Dolorosa,
Bethlehem and with our family and group from Kehillat
Israel we visited Yad Vashem.

Our guide through Yad Vashem was a Holocaust
survivor in her late 70s. How she was able to guide
groups through the museum after having lived and
survived the concentration camps is beyond
comprehension. She felt that her being there added to
the authenticity of the exhibit.

At the end of the tour she and I embraced and I said
to her, "We are still here in spite of all this".

Then, just our family, Marsi, Chayim, Mandi,
Molli, Daniel, Norma and I went to Yad Vashem's
"The Valley of the Communities,"

a massive 2.5-acre monument literally dug out of natural bedrock. Over 5,000 names of communities are engraved on the stone walls. Each name recalls a Jewish community that had existed for hundreds of years, until the Holocaust. For the inhabitants, each community constituted an entire world. Today, in most cases, nothing remains there but the name.

Daniel, Mandi, me, Norma, Chayim and Marsi at the Valley of the Communities

We found the stone representing Darmstadt, where my mother was born and where she had lived. We found the town in Czechoslovakia where Chayim's mother was born as well as Worme, the oldest Jewish cemetery in Germany, which we had visited when we were in Frankfurt.

I have snorkeled the Great Barrier Reef in Australia, which was fantastic. We have walked on the Great Wall of China in several locations; saw the Terracotta Warriors in Xian, China, crossed the Continental

Divide, Montana, in a 1923 Ford open top Touring car, restored by the Ford company, walked on the Columbia glacier, seen the glaciers in Alaska, been to the top of the Eiffel Tower, seen the Coliseum in Rome, the Parthenon in Greece, the Leaning Tower of Pisa, been through the canals in Venice, seen the Taj Mahal in India both in the daytime as well as in the moonlight, enjoyed Whistler Mountain, Lake Louise and The Butchart Gardens in Canada, explored the Grand Canyon, Bryce Canyon, where I toured on horseback, Zion and Kings Canyon National Parks, Yosemite National Park and Copper Canyon in Mexico. I've searched for the Loch Ness Monster in Scotland, spent a month in South Africa and a week at the magnificent Kruger National Park. I've listened to the Mormon Tabernacle choir at the Temple in Ogdon, Utah, walked into the bowels of the earth at the magnificent Carlsbad Caverns in New Mexico. I've been inside of a pyramid and in the Valley of the Kings in Egypt, and I've seen the Hiroshima Peace Memorial Museum. We visited the Expectamus Dominium cemetery in Buenos Aires, Devils Island in France, where Captain Dreyfus was incarcerated for treason, and then later found not guilty, transited the Panama Canal numerous times, and prior to becoming commercialized, last year we visited Cuba.

Some of these places are considered to be the Seven Wonders of the World. But are they really? In my opinion, the true Wonders of the World are the birth of one's children, grandchildren, and great grandchildren, hearing them laugh, seeing them smile and play, feeling their hugs, and enjoying their love.

These wonders can't be made or bought by man.

Chapter 61-Conclusion

I am ever so grateful to have survived and lived to see my family resurrected. We are blessed to be welcomed into all our children's and granddaughter's home as they are in ours.

Joel operates the Bargain Center and his four children are all adults. Amy, the oldest, lives in Chicago with her husband Jake and both are working for Aramark. On October 29th, 2016 they welcomed their first baby, Emerson Lee. She is our first great grandchild.

Daniel lives in Santa Barbara and is a photojournalist.

The twins, Jeffrey and Janine, both live and work in San Diego.

Going to Bob's house in Willits, Northern California is always an experience. His home sits on the side of a mountain on a 10-acre plot of pine trees. He always has at least two or three dogs, a few cats and a bird there.

Last summer when we were there, he set up a giant tepee and held a prayer meeting that was attended by about 30 people of all ages. It lasted all night, (we didn't), and was followed the next morning with a barbecue feast.

Ted is vice President, Marketing Dental Specialties for Henry Schein Company. He lives in Coto de Caza, about an hour and 15 minutes north of our house, with his wife Niki, 12 year old son Sammy and 4 year old Kate. They are our two youngest grandchildren. Sam plays Pop Warner football, and we love going to his games.

Their vacation home is at Big Bear Lake in the San Bernardino Mountains. We have our own suite on the lower level. Katie always wants us to come to "her cabin." I ask her, "Where is the cabin?" And she says, "Up the hill." She also loves to stand on Ted's lap and help drive their boat. With FaceTime, we keep in touch almost every evening.

We usually spend the High Holy Days at Marsi and Chayim's home in Pacific Palisades. We attend services at Kehillat Israel (KI) where we are members and where Chayim is the cantor. Mandi, their oldest daughter is an Israeli citizen, living a bit outside of Tel Aviv and going to college. She inherited her father's voice and sings like an angel. Molli attends public high school in Los Angeles. She loves music and dancing.

I am accepted, respected and loved by my foster family, my schoolmates, the many life-time friends I have made here in San Diego, as well as the hundreds of passengers from all over the world whom we have met on our cruises.

The terrific staff on the Crystal World Cruises has without a doubt enriched our lives. All, from the captain to the housekeepers, treat Norma and me like royalty. We adore our World Cruise hostess, Stacey Huston, whom we met on our first World Cruise in 2009. Several times she has read parts of this book on the morning show. We always love being with our World Cruise directors, Rick Spath and Gary Hunter, also a ventriloquist, whom we have known for many years. Gary chose me to be his dummy on the 2009 World Cruise and it was a ball. He gave me a DVD of the performance. On our first day of the 2015 World Cruise, a passenger remembered me as being the dummy. Everyone who sees the DVD cracks up.

We can always count on having our regular Bridge instructors, Jeff and Ginny, who make everyone feel welcomed and continue to try to teach old dogs' new tricks year after year.

Joe Kita, the memoir-writing instructor on the World Cruises, whom I first met on the 2014 World Cruise, has been a tremendous help to me. He inspires passengers to write, not only memoirs but also anything one wishes to write. Near the end of each of the five world cruise segments, many people on the ship gather together to listen to some of the stories that were written by passengers while at sea.

It is great to stay healthy and live to a ripe old age but there is a definite down side. As one gets older more and more friends and family members pass away. It's like building a stone wall that continues to be built at one end while the original end crumbles away.

That's life; it's what you make it. Make it good. You only have one to live.

Made in the USA
Monee, IL
01 July 2021

72697456R00164